FOREVER ATHLETE

Connect with Your True Identity Daily

RD,

Thank you for everything this far. Your
Light, energy, and support changes the game
for people around you. Keep Shining Brother!

Keegan Sawyer

A Collection of Stories from
PEAK PERFORMERS

Self -n- DAYS
Publish 30   This Is The Year For
             Your New Book

Published by *Self Publish -N- 30 Days*

© Copyright 2022

Printed in the United States of America

ISBN: 979-8-42256-076-9

1. Nonfiction 2. Sports 3. Entrepreneurship

Forever Athlete: Connect with Your True Identity Daily

Contributing Authors: Cory Camp, Joe Rinaldi, Darci Smith, Dr. Matt Wiest, Dephanie Adeyemi, David Karasek, Ellen Renk, Rachel Breton, Nikki Kett, Sarah Neal, Chloe Maleski, Cody Allen, Erika Fay, Sarah Fritsche, Gavin McHale, Kim Brady, Sarah Williams, and Keegan LaMar.

TABLE OF CONTENTS

TABLE OF CONTENTS

INTRODUCTION

"What you do for a living doesn't define you, it is just an expression of who you are."

— Cory Camp

If you're reading this, you probably spent most of your youth and developmental years identifying as an athlete. Maybe you routinely introduced yourself to new acquaintances as, "Hi, I'm _____, the *insert sport here. *" I know that's how a majority of my life went. It's that way for a lot of athletes.

So, when the final buzzer sounds and the crowd empties out for the last time, it can be tough to take it all in. It is a challenge to process your identity beyond being an athlete when that's all you've known your whole life.

No guest speaker talk can really prepare you for the journey that you undertake when you walk away from athletics. It doesn't matter if it's on your own terms or not; eventually, we have to discover our true selves beyond being an athlete.

Sports are great because, in many ways, they give us a playground to discover ourselves on. Sports are a container to try, fail, get back up, dust off the dirt, and try again. Sports are a beautiful thing, aren't they? As athletes, we wouldn't be who we are today without having experienced all that we did. It can be tough to find your true self beyond your sport,

1

especially when that was what allowed you to find yourself in the first place.

Talk about a serious catch-22.

Where do we start in solving this identity crisis, and how do we find purpose beyond our athletic talents and abilities? It begins in the language that we choose to use. I have a strong distaste toward the word "former" in reference to anything but I am bothered by "former athlete" especially. To me, this term conveys that the person we've been up until this moment is no longer valid.

That couldn't be further than the truth. Who would we be without those experiences? The idea of packing up who we are and tucking it into a box for storage, just to collect dust in our parents' basement, doesn't sit right with me. I know I'm not alone in this. The stories in this book, told by others who have faced the same dilemma, prove what can happen when you shift to identifying as a Forever Athlete who lives life outside the box and isn't afraid to grow.

This is a collection of the stories of high performers across all industries and from many different backgrounds, who have chosen to answer the call of embodying the Forever Athlete mindset and identity.

The beauty is that there is no single way to become a Forever Athlete. The journey of finding yourself beyond what you do will look different for everyone, just as all athletes develop in their sports in unique ways.

However, there is one underlying theme you will see. Each of these people started with a decision to grow beyond their current circumstances. It was a decision to keep moving forward, often despite what was happening around them. You made the same decision when picking up this book, despite living in a world of constant distraction.

This project is intended to get your gears turning toward finding your true self each day, to take the limits out of your life and allow you to play your game again. Think back to when you first discovered sports, and all the wonderful things it allowed you to experience. Wasn't it a blast? The focus was on fun and community, not on the pressures to perform up to a certain standard. Now that we are on the other side, it can be tough to have fun again when we hold such high expectations of ourselves.

" The beauty is that there is no single way to become a Forever Athlete. "

Our expectation of what life should look like is preventing us from seeing the beauty of how life can be beyond sports. It took me a long time to learn that high standards and fun aren't mutually exclusive to one another. It took me an even longer time to be okay with having free time on my hands.

Maybe you experienced this shift within sports, struggling to find joy in the daily grind because it was your job. For some, it goes as far as your self-worth becoming directly tied to the outcome of your performance. That can be a dangerous place to perform and come back from, but if that's you, don't fear. There is hope. I know because that was me.

The current system is set up to have you believe you can't have your cake and eat it too, that you have to wait until a certain age, a certain level of financial freedom, to live the life you want to truly be living. What if you could start living that life today? Not by pretending you're someone you're not, but by being you? This book aims to show you how.

Being a Forever Athlete means actively seeking out ways to grow, explore, and find freedom, all while playing a good game of life. It means bringing the fight to the world, not sitting back and waiting for a handout. You can do this with a big grin on your face, knowing that you are being your authentic self.

If you're looking for the easy way out, this book isn't for you. But I know, as an athlete, you're no stranger to hard work. This serves as a steppingstone that will allow you to tap into your true identity daily.

What would happen in your life if you chose to start shifting into the Forever Athlete identity? If you made a decision to tap into your true self? Every. Single. Day.

I don't have the answer for you there. Only you do, and it's locked away inside. This book is intended to help you start uncovering those answers. Through other Forever Athletes' stories, you can gain clarity on your own story, and the journey you have yet to take to discover yourself beyond sports.

The lesson in this book is that no matter where you're at, no matter how down bad you might be right now, there is a way forward. We tap into our true identity through every decision we make, and you can do the same through the wisdom shared within the pages of this book.

I already know you're not like most people. You're here reading this with the desire to improve your life when you could be doing anything else. That drive and ambition to be better says a lot about you already.

We are all one team here, so let's get moving forward together.

I'll see you there,
Cory

Chapter 1

FINDING FLOW AS A FISH OUT OF WATER BY CORY CAMP

One last race stood between me and retirement. I was on the pool deck at Virginia Tech, waiting for my final swim. This would not only be my last swim for the University of Delaware but as a swimmer in general. A journey of self-improvement and discovery that started when I nearly drowned at four years old was about to come to an end. Eighteen years later, here I stood getting ready to swim one last mile, a long-time staple event for me. After countless hours staring at the black line on pool bottoms all over the country, fifteen minutes stood between me and the *real world*.

It was a world that, honestly, I had been dreading for a while.

I hit the warmup pool for one last shake-out, getting both my mind and body right to perform under pressure like I always had. It was the final day of the Colonial Athletic Association Conference Championships, and out of my four years as a college athlete, I'd always performed my best on the biggest stage here. While the first few days were nowhere close to where I performed in prior years, I was ready to go out with a bang.

Doesn't every athlete want to go out on top? Ride off into the sunset having ended their story on their terms? I viewed my final race, the

1650 freestyle, as my opportunity to write the last chapter in my book of who I was as a swimmer.

At ten years old, I found distance swimming and never looked back, excelling more the longer the race was. This was the perfect race for me to end things on; I was ready to right the ship and leave an exclamation point at the close of my career.

Stepping behind the blocks and listening to my name get announced for the final time, I turned to my dad and gave him one last nod. It was go-time. I stepped up on the starting block, clapped two times, and locked in. Nothing else in the world mattered.

Take your mark, beep.

I exploded off the blocks into the same dive I'd perfected over the years. I felt the familiar rush of cutting through the water, and muscle memory took over; I was in my element. Those first moments in the water were the best part of my race that night. Every other piece fell apart fast. I remember my mind drifting elsewhere by the halfway mark, questioning when the physical pain my body was experiencing would be over. Every muscle in my body seemed to be on fire. The longer the race went on, the worse I felt.

I touched the wall for the final time to see the scoreboard light up a time of 15:51.66, and an eighth-place finish. This was the lowest I had ever placed during my college career. My world came crashing down in that instant. My final race, my defining moment, ended up slower than I had ever been in six years prior. How could this happen to me?

As athletes, we are raised to believe it's all about how you did in your current performance, not previous ones. It's all about who showed up on that night when it counted the most. So, it was hard not to feel like this last race defined who I was more than all of the ones that preceded it. I remember a wave of emotions pouring over me at that moment. The ever-present question for me now became, *who am I beyond a swimmer now that this is over?*

In the swimming world, we refer to the newly-retired as "swammers." I certainly felt like one that night, and let me tell you, it did not feel good. I felt washed up and burned out, a total shell of my former self. This was not how it was supposed to end. I found myself in the locker room with the other newly-dubbed swammers a few hours later, popping bottles of champagne. It was a celebration I couldn't help but feel was hollow based on how I had performed.

This moment kicked off the start of the next chapter of my life, but I couldn't shake the feeling that a piece of me died that night in the pool. Without the feedback and structure that swimming provided me, I found my world starting to unravel around me more and more.

Returning to campus, I was finally a college NARP (non-athletic regular person), an identity that I previously couldn't wait for because of the freedom it would provide me, but suddenly found myself struggling to connect with. That last semester was supposed to be the best semester of my college life because I finally had free time, yet I had so many questions buzzing through my head that I couldn't focus.

My original plan post-swim was to go into physical therapy school. It was something I had been pursuing since my senior year of high school, and I was sure that it would just work out without much effort on my part. If a bad final race was the first blow, getting denied from PT school felt like a ton of bricks crashing down on my head. It felt like I was finding more questions than answers. *What was I going to do now?*

More importantly, what was going to make me happy? What was going to make me feel like me again? I desperately wanted to know the answer to these questions. Sports are simple. You have a clear-cut ladder in front of you to climb. Attend X number of practices, work your ass off, and get rewarded. If not in that exact moment, at least you got feedback on what to do next. But what do you do when there is no next meet or practice to implement that feedback? Even worse, what do you do when you don't even know what sort of feedback to look for anymore?

As athletes, we understand that our best performance can always be improved. We look for new foods to eat, supplements to take, or new training methods, all to get a leg up on our past selves. It can be maddening at times, but that's the life of an athlete. At least in the container of sports, you had a direction in which to aim. I found myself lost, without purpose, knowing I could work hard, but what for? When we aren't in tune with our highest self, we experience dissatisfaction with our current situation. The more out of alignment we are, the more frustrated we begin to feel.

Happiness, I've learned, is actually simple. See below:

Expectation   Reality
X   X

Happiness is measured by how close our expectations of ourselves are to our reality of ourselves. This is to say, how we view both of these determines our happiness in life. When swimming ended, my expectation was that I would get into PT school, move to Philly to stay close with the girl I was dating at the time, and be working a good six-figure job within the next few years. One by one, those expectations were shattered, and not in a good way. No PT school. No more girlfriend. An entry-level sales job was the only thing available to me.

My expectations couldn't have been further from my reality, and I was downright miserable because of it. So, I tried to alter my reality, turning to the best way I knew how: escaping it. I found myself a frequent flyer of the bars, something I had never had the chance to do as a swimmer. I wanted to redefine myself.

The answers I was searching for I thought could be found at the bottom of a Captain Morgan 100 proof. Alcohol is a funny thing; we search for ourselves in it, but it only widens the gap between ourselves and what we want to find. It numbs the immediate pain yet prolongs whatever it is we are hoping to forget.

I know this because it got to the point where I would finish a fifth of whiskey at the pregame, drinking like a fish to numb the disconnect of no longer being a fish in the pool.

A vicious cycle was introduced into my life when I started my first job in sales. I was a mortgage refinancer, which in my eyes was a far less sexy job title than a physical therapist (again, expectation vs reality). I took the athlete approach of showing up early, staying late, and putting in the extra reps to get better each day. It worked for a while, and I started to finally gain traction and financial success. But then more began to be expected of me, and it started to feel like a never-ending energy-suck.

This went on for months until I got an email from the parent of some kids I had previously given swim lessons. She was wondering if I was still in the area and if I would be able to teach her boys again on the weekends. With the little free time I had, I felt a calling to say yes to this opportunity. Before I knew it, my Sundays filled with giving individual lessons to families that had heard I was coaching again.

I started to notice that I felt the most like myself on Sundays, and I dreaded heading back into work from Monday to Saturday. A few months later, I decided to quit my job in the mortgage industry. I wanted to feel like me again: that kid who enjoyed his time in the pool, who found excitement in the mundane task of staring at a black line. I couldn't stomach the gap any longer, so I decided to take the plunge. I went from struggling to stay afloat to finding my flow again by listening to my heart for the first time in years.

Looking back, this decision was the first one I truly made for myself since my swimming career had ended. Everything up to that point had been to prove something to those around me. In the process of trying to prove to my teammates I had it figured out on my first try, or prove to my parents I was successful by the amount of money coming into my bank account, I had denied my heart what it actually wanted in favor of impressing others.

This shift in my priorities led me to become a summer swim coach. *But Cory, isn't that a step back?* Just wait, it gets better. I also went back to lifeguarding. There I was, at twenty-three years old, with a college degree and seven school records, spending eight hours a day in a fucking lifeguard chair watching geriatric swimmers go back and forth at a crawl.

You might be thinking, *I don't see how this is the story of someone always moving forward toward their true self.* Trust me, in the moment I was struggling to see that too, but stay with me.

I used that time in the chair to sit and think, for the first time in years, about what I really wanted. What were my true expectations of myself? Not those placed on me by society or the people around me, but the expectations I came up with on my own. I realized all I really wanted was to make an impact in someone's life. It was a trait I admired in all of my role models.

So how was I going to do that while coaching and sitting in a chair watching other people swim for forty hours a week? I decided that I could only do it by changing my reality while enjoying the chapter of life I was in. One day, an idea popped into my head. *What if I started a year-round club swim team?* The club I was at had the perfect space for it, and it was never used, so I went to the operations director later that day and pitched him my idea. He loved it and told me to come up with a formal business plan so we could iron out the details.

I had no idea what that meant, but I said I'd have it to him by the end of the week. Thank God for Google. In three days, I wrote my first-ever business proposal for a learn-to-swim clinic and year-round age group program. I knew this was the next step to imparting the wisdom swimming had given me to the next generation, and I couldn't have been more excited. That was my whole pitch. I was the perfect person to do this job. I was so confident in it, and they saw that as well. They agreed to rent me the space for free, something I didn't see coming.

Within our first year of operation, I had thirty kids in the age group program, and more than fifty kids attending our clinics. I hired a full-time assistant and we were rolling. I had stepped away from sales, surrendering the need to let financial success be the only metric I measured myself by, and here I was, less than a year later, making more than I ever had in sales. I had followed my heart and true passion, and my success was by no means a coincidence.

I became impact-driven, on a mission to change the lives of those I had the opportunity to work with. This began to extend beyond the pool when I got my personal training certification. That, I had decided, was my next calling, something I could step into in addition to the swim groups I was running. Before I knew it, I was named the assistant fitness director at the same club. In a matter of a year, I went from sitting in a lifeguard chair to now being responsible for a team of fifty people. How did this happen?

For the first time since swimming, I felt like I had that ladder framework and was able to put my head down and just be me again. I wasn't worried about the outcome, only with how I could show up and impact those directly in front of me each day. It didn't matter if it was the three-year-old learning how to blow bubbles, or the eighty-three-year-old I was helping rehab from back surgery. I was finding fulfillment in each task I was able to do each day.

Things were finally rolling for me, it seemed. Around the time I got promoted, a friend of mine asked me to be a guest on his podcast, *Pregame Conversations*. Not usually one to be outspoken (I was always more of an introverted leader, someone who would let my actions show you what to do rather than tell you), I thought, *what the heck, why not?* Little did I know, this was the planting of a seed that would grow into my current career.

After adjusting to the awkwardness of having a microphone in my face, I opened up and was able to let the true me shine throughout the course of the show. I was able to surrender to the flow of the conversation rather than simply reading off the pre-scripted material, and I was blown away by some of the feedback I got as other friends listened, and some asked if I had considered starting my own show.

It had never occurred to me that I had something worth sharing publicly at that level. I was perfectly content serving the clientele at the club. But again, something inside of me felt called to give it a try. About a month later, I bought a plug-in microphone, wrote out my swimming journey, and within a few days I had put together what would be *The Athletic Mindset's* first episode. I knew from the start I didn't want this podcast to be limited as simply a platform to share my experiences with mental performance. I wanted to pick the brains of the world's elite athletes and coaches.

After releasing a solo first episode, I started tapping into the network of other athletes I had connected with over the years. It became a great opportunity to sit down and have deeper conversations with them. I learned very quickly that there is tremendous power in networking with a purpose. Intentional conversations with good people go a long way in building everyone up and progressing further in life.

When the first episode was released in September 2019, I had no idea what to expect from the audience, or if I would even *have* a substantial audience. While it's easy to look back now and see over 100 episodes released, it's been a slow-growing process. I was beyond nervous the first time I sat down with an Olympian, but just like anything, the more you do it the calmer you're able to be.

I also realized something else while speaking to over 100 high-level athletes, many of whom are featured in this book. They are all human, and we have more in common than we might originally have thought.

At the time, I viewed the podcast as a cool side project to what I was building at the club. I had no expectations for it; I simply enjoyed having in-depth conversations with interesting people and sharing them with an audience.

However, as the months went by, I started to feel like my growth in my role at the club was being stunted. I was quickly approaching my ceiling there and running out of hours in the day to scale my impact the way I wanted to. You know that feeling when the training group or team you were on was great, but they weren't going to allow you to take your game to the next level? That's where I was in early 2020.

When March 2020 hit and the world shut down, I was provided some time to sit and think about what was next for me. What would be the next "team" I joined that would push me to continue growing outside of my comfort zone?

Luckily, the early-pandemic days meant I had a lot of time on my hands. In addition to producing the podcast, I had been studying for a mental performance mastery certification, which I saw as an opportunity to formalize my education around mindset coaching. I finally had the time to finish that up. Once I added that to my toolbox, I was faced with figuring out what I actually wanted to do with it.

I ended up spending the last week of March creating a whole curriculum for current athletes to master their own mental performance. I called it "Athletic Mindset Coaching," and by the first week of April, I had fifty age group swimmers enrolled in my first nine-week course. I found a new level of excitement helping these young swimmers navigate the unique challenges they were facing with no practices or meets for the first time in their lives.

They were struggling to discover whom they were beyond simply being athletes; it was the question that had hit me like ton of bricks years prior, and now I was able to help them through it. It's the very same question that inspired this book and the company I founded, Forever Athlete.

I made close to no money from the time I invested into that program and the kids I worked with, but I was absolutely lit up about the work we explored together. This sparked newer, more complex conversations on the podcast around this topic of identity, mental health, and our performance. I was noticing more and more, with every athlete I talked to, that there was a lack of community and space for these conversations, let alone any true guidance on what to do from there.

This curiosity was being met with something I was truly passionate about, and I knew I was on to something. Throughout the years, I had heard of personal development and self-help books but had never really connected with the way they spoke to me. I think part of that was ego and stubbornness, thinking, *why would this work for me? They don't know me.*

Even having gone to therapy over the years, I still felt as though a relatable game plan for the future was lacking. I set out with an insatiable hunger to better understand how we as humans operate and bridge the gap between academia and the world we actually live in. I felt like an athlete learning a new skill.

Better yet, I felt like a kid again. I started to use any free time I had to come up with experiments to test the theories I was reading or heard about on podcasts. I tried new routines and new challenges to push my mind and body, such as a 5:00 am running streak. I dabbled with journaling, meditating, and true vision boarding. I found the routines that served me best showed themselves the more mindful I became of my own needs. Instead of forcing life, I devised a playbook so to speak that's allowed me to call the right play for the right moment.

Then one day it hit me. What if we were going about this whole lifestyle transition thing completely wrong? What if, just as when we got into sports, we did it not for the fame, accolades, and glory, but for the community, fun, and personal growth? Isn't that what really drew most of us into our sport in the first place? I didn't start swimming with the intention to become a D1 swimmer; I started because I enjoyed my time in the water with great people around me.

Somewhere along our journey on the playground of sports, wires get crossed and we can end up losing ourselves in the process. The focus shifts away from fun (an internal motivator) to winning (an external motivator), and when that shift happens, it's hard to disassociate who we are from the results we are getting. The external expectations only get higher as you climb the ladder of progress and development in your abilities.

The breakthrough I had was simple: what happens when we shift our focus back to fun and enjoyment? To say yes to ourselves instead of no, and listen to our intuition? I realized this was the hypothesis I had been testing ever since I left my job as a mortgage refinancer. I also realized that it's something we could all benefit from in every aspect of our lives.

Instead of buying into the box that the world tries to put us in by labeling us as former athletes, what if we bought into the idea of living life outside the box as Forever Athletes?

> "What if, just as when we got into sports, we did it not for the fame, accolades, and glory, but for the community, fun, and personal growth?"

These are the questions that served as the launchpad for this book you're holding in your hands. These are the questions that I continually ask myself each day. Since March 2020, my life has changed drastically in some of the best ways possible. I quit my job at the club and became a founder of a company that makes an impact each day.

I moved to Los Angeles to live on the beach with two of my best friends from early swimming days, and I now run a global company that serves athletes who were just like me, with no flow in their life and no idea where they wanted to go. The secret sauce to my journey has been allowing myself intentional time to slow down and listen to what my body, mind, and the universe are telling me.

It might seem like the trajectory of my life as of late has been a linear rocket into the sky, but I have had my fair share of ups and downs. You know, as an athlete at heart, that the road is anything but smooth. If you're going through a struggle right now, just know that in the midst of the storm is where our best skills are developed. Just how you had to train all season to prepare for the championship game, life has its own seasons to it.

The beauty is you don't have to go through that struggle alone. With every open, honest, and vulnerable conversation I've had throughout the years, I've only grown more in tune with my true self. It's also brought great people into my life and allowed me to become more connected with those I care about.

We are all running around trying to figure out who we are in this world, and what our role is for those around us. In doing so, we miss the most important question: who are we for ourselves? The more clarity I've gained about that question throughout this journey, the better I've been able to show up in the roles I do have. As athletes, we tend to hyper-focus on the external work ethic, because that's what we are most familiar with. We were trained to work out, but did not get a lot of instruction on how to work *in*.

Working in allows us to feel what we need to, process what is going on, and better understand the root of why we are feeling this way. Answering the question of who you are for yourself is the jumping-off point to working in. It's the start of a limitless journey into the abundant flow of your life, and it only begins when you release the need to impress those around you. Over the years, I've learned that working this in can be done through various methods: long aerobic exercise, mindfulness practices, meditation, reading. The only prerequisite to working in is that you must create the space and be open to going there.

The more that I work inward, the more I discover that I have always had everything I need inside to validate me. It's allowed me to create my own flow from my own source. When you allow your expectations and reality to meet in the middle, you say yes to your true self. In doing so, happiness comes from the most powerful source of all: **you.**

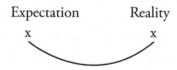

Expectation   Reality

Source: You

I've been able to get where I am today because I learned to stop placing so much emphasis on how the world perceives me. Instead, I focus on how I can show up, for myself, every single day. What can I do on a daily basis to further myself, my happiness, and the impact I have on the people around me? So, I'll leave you with this.

How will you show up for yourself today?

ABOUT CORY

Cory Camp uncovered his passion for making a difference in other people's lives as a swim coach, emphasizing growth over perfection with those he coached. Now, Cory is the founder of Forever Athlete, LLC, a company focused on the conscious connection of athletes through flow state and community.

As a writer, speaker, podcast host, and coach, Cory is known for facilitating flow for his clients by peeling away limiting beliefs and tapping into their inner higher self. His positive, in-the-trenches-with-you style propels those he works with to achieve balance in their everyday lives.

Cory is a Forever Athlete, certified mental performance coach, and a certified strength and conditioning coach. He is a former national-level swimmer at the University of Delaware, where he holds seven school records. Cory also hosts *Forever Athlete Radio Podcast*, a show dedicated to looking at the role our mindset plays in our everyday life.

You can reach out to Cory and join the Forever Athlete Network community at www.foreverathletela.com or cory@foreverathletela. com.

Chapter 2

LIKE IT'S ON FILM
BY JOE RINALDI

I wouldn't be who I am without sports, but they don't define me.

Let me take you back to the beginning.

Thanks to my dad, I fell in love with the sport of baseball from a very young age. He taught me everything he knew about the sport and coached almost every team that I played on. Growing up, most of my clothing was covered in that red diamond dirt that stained everything it came into contact with. I spent more time swinging a bat than I did anything else, and I was driven to make baseball a lasting part of my life.

However, at the age of ten, all of that changed. I experienced an abrupt loss of sight and was diagnosed with Best Disease, a genetic condition that results in the progressive loss of central eyesight. From that point on, baseball, among other things, became very difficult for me. Following a few too many baseballs to the face, I was forced to make the difficult decision to give up the game that I loved.

With baseball out of the picture, I turned my attention to football, a sport where poor eyesight could be made up with intelligence, work ethic, and brute force. Unlike baseball, which required tracking a small white ball moving at high speeds, football was more of a physical sport where hand-eye coordination wasn't needed to the same degree. While

I missed baseball throughout my teenage years, I soon fell in love with football, and it quickly became a part of my athletic identity.

Four years of football at Westfield High School in New Jersey taught me a lot. The athletic tradition in town was one of excellence, and it was a big deal to play varsity football. Throughout my time in the program, our teams were filled with athletes who were all striving toward greatness, and that was reflected in our frequent and challenging practices.

The coaches in the program cared deeply about helping the team win, but they also had a vested interest in helping my teammates and I develop into better people. In many ways, the experiences I had and the people I got to know through high school sports shaped me into the person I am today.

Following high school, I attended Bucknell University, where I did not intend to play football. However, after a few weeks at school, I realized that something was missing; I had never been in a season of life without sport, and I realized I didn't want to be.

With the help and guidance of my high school coach, I ended up walking onto the football team at Bucknell University. Within a matter of weeks, things fell into place. I found a rhythm and I was feeling like myself. Everything was going well until I made a tackle and immediately knew that something was wrong.

I stood up, adjusted my helmet, and realized that the world looked different than it had just a few seconds before. I had suddenly lost a significant portion of my eyesight. My heart dropped into my stomach as I ran to the sidelines to tell my coach what was happening. Disoriented and disheartened, I left the stadium that evening not knowing what the future held. In the coming days, after consulting a few specialists, my football career came to an abrupt end.

To this day, I miss playing football, and I don't think that feeling will ever go away. While my time as an athlete came to an unexpected end long before I would've liked, the game taught me more than I could have ever asked for, and my experiences helped make me the person I am today: a person who follows a relentless drive to pursue their fullest potential while lifting others up along the way.

The lessons I learned during my high school football career, as well as my time in college, transcend sport and continue to drive me in my career and everyday life. While the lessons that follow are not exhaustive, I believe that any athlete, whether in the midst of their career or beyond, can relate to and find value in what I've learned from the sport that I love.

1. Football taught me what it means to make a commitment and be disciplined.

To practice discipline means adhering to a pattern of behavior, a promise, or a commitment all the time—especially when you don't feel like it. Discipline is about creating and honoring a commitment, and football is one of the biggest commitments I've ever made.

I remember the summers during high school when I worked a full-time job as a camp counselor during the day, and then rode my bike to football summer conditioning workouts in the evening. I can recall how physically and mentally tired I was after supervising children at work each day, and how even though I never initially felt like it, I had to make the conscious daily decision to put aside one exhaustion for another. I gave my best effort, even when I didn't want to, because that was a commitment I had made long ago, not only to myself but to my coaches and teammates as well.

The discipline and commitment that football taught me have translated to every aspect of my life and become part of who I am. I've come to understand that commitment is a dedicated act of love and endurance. Whether it's in sports, school, relationships, or anything else, find the things worth committing to and then give them your best.

"Commitment means doing what you said you were going to do long after the mood you said it in has left you."

— Orebela Gbenga

2. Football taught me that persistent hard work always pays off.

I'm grateful to have been born with some level of coordination and athleticism. However, I was middle of the pack when it came to natural football abilities. I'm grateful for that because it forced me to work.

> **"**
> The lessons I learned during my high school football career, as well as my time in college, transcend sport and continue to drive me in my career and everyday life.
> **"**

As a freshman in high school, I didn't get much playing time, and that ignited something in me. I used the summer following that year to put in some serious work (I'm talking about flipping tires, pushing sleds, and doing solo wind sprints in ninety-degree weather after everyone else went home), and that earned me varsity playing time as a sophomore. Still not satisfied, I continued to push past my preconceived limits, and it paid dividends. I started a few varsity games as a junior and, with continued hard work, started both ways for my entire senior season. The hard work had paid off.

Throughout high school football, relentless effort and drive put me in a position to attack goals and get where I wanted to be. The challenging part about hard work is that the results aren't always immediate. In other words, there's often lag time between effort and outcome, and that can be discouraging. I learned that to get the best results, effort also requires patience, persistence, endurance, and a strong driving force. In all that you do, be persistent with your effort.

"A river cuts through rock not because of its power, but because of its persistence."

— Jim Watkins

3. Football taught me how to be a great teammate.

Being part of a team means working together with a group of people toward a common goal. While that statement is true, it's missing something. Being a good teammate goes beyond working toward a common goal; being a *great* teammate transcends sports. It means supporting others, picking them up when they're down, and holding others accountable for their actions. It means leading by example, being honest, and giving it your all, on the field, in the classroom, and everywhere else.

I had a memorable experience while playing youth football that will stick with me for life. I got into trouble at practice for doing something I shouldn't have been doing, and my coach at the time made the entire team run laps as punishment. However, before we ran, he told us that as teammates, we win together, lose together, have fun together, and get in trouble together. The lesson was that it's bigger than us. In sport, but also in life, we find ourselves as part of various teams, with groups of people to whom we are committed.

Whether it's a football team, a friendship, a marriage, or anything else, when we commit to other people, we win together, lose together, have fun together, and get in trouble together. Life is so much bigger than us, and part of what makes life meaningful is sharing the highs and the lows with the people around you. In all areas of life, strive to be a great teammate.

"Teamwork is the ability to work together toward a common vision. The ability to direct individual accomplishments toward organizational objectives. It is the fuel that allows common people to attain uncommon results."
— Andrew Carnegie

4. Football taught me to play to the whistle and run through the finish line.
My high school football program was never the biggest, the fastest, or the strongest, but we were almost always the best conditioned. What this meant was that when the fourth quarter came around, when the other team was tired and slowing down, we were still heating up and ready to go. As a result, we were able to finish strong and dominate the game late on a consistent basis.

Through football, I've learned time and time again that it doesn't always matter how you start, but it does always matter how you finish. It has shown me that endurance with purpose is a winning recipe on the field and in life. I've been able to make a habit out of finishing strong, and that's served me well. In sports and in life, run through the line and finish strong.

> *"Most people never run far enough on their first wind to find out they've got a second. Give your dreams all you've got and you'll be amazed at the energy that comes out of you."*
>
> — William James

Each of these lessons has stuck with me thus far, long after I stepped off the field for the last time. However, there is one concept, that more than the rest, echoes deep in my core:

5. Football taught me how to be a better person.
If you've ever played football at a competitive level, you know what it's like to watch a film. If you've never played football, let me break it down for you.

Teams will watch a film (practices/games) together, and coaches use these sessions to provide constructive criticism. As you sit in a room surrounded by your teammates and coaches, every single mistake is up on the big screen for everyone to see. There is nowhere to run and nowhere to hide.

Film sessions are constructive in nature, but sometimes you simply get ripped apart, in front of your peers nonetheless, and that doesn't feel good at all. Through all of my years playing football, despite my fair share of embarrassing moments, I was able to notice a common theme threaded throughout every film session.

It didn't matter how much talent you had or how good you were. There were only two things that really mattered:

Did you do your job?

Did you give your best effort?

Knowing that every move, every step, and every breath would be on film, something inevitably happened: I began to play every play like someone was watching, because … they were. Knowing that my play would be put up on the big screen for all to see took away every excuse. It gave me no choice but to put forth my best effort all the time because I had to be completely accountable for all of my actions. This sense of ownership made me a better football player, a better teammate, and most importantly, a better person. So, I began to think…

If the thought of being watched by others made me more accountable for my actions, why couldn't that same concept carry over to all areas of life?

The end of my football career seemed to coincide with the beginning of a more serious spiritual chapter of my life. I began to grow my relationship with God, and I became more aware of the fact that God is watching over me always, and in the end, I am accountable to Him. While my faith plays a large role in my life, this isn't an attempt to push my beliefs on you; in fact, it's far from it. I want to share my personal experience so that you can gain an appreciation for how this lesson from sports has translated outside of football to the rest of my life.

Regardless of your spiritual background and whether or not you believe you are being watched; I want to urge you to try your best to live every second of every day as if someone is watching over you. In other words, treat every "play" of every day like it will be part of a film session.

By living life under the true or hypothetical pretense that your actions will be seen by someone else, you can be accountable for your actions and live with integrity. This last lesson is about doing the right thing even when it's inconvenient, especially when it's hard, and regardless of whether anybody else will see it.

Every decision you make, both in public and in private, ultimately affects the people around you. That's because every decision today changes who you become tomorrow. When you leave the field, go out and live a life that you'd be proud to put on film.

> *"Be more concerned with your character than your reputation, because your character is what you really are, while your reputation is merely what others think you are... The true test of a man's character is what he does when no one is watching."*
>
> — John Wooden

I want to express my gratitude for your attention. Reflecting and writing have always been valuable to me, and I hope that my words have been valuable to you as well. Contributing to this collection of athletic journeys has reminded me how precious my time playing football truly was and how I wish I could go back and play just one more game. Let that be the last lesson. In sport and in life, don't take anything for granted. Leave everything out on the field and play every game like it's your last because someday, it will be.

ABOUT JOE

Joe Rinaldi, PT, DPT, is a doctor of physical therapy, performance coach, writer, and speaker who resides in Philadelphia, Pennsylvania with his wife and best friend, Michaela. He currently works with a wide range of athletes across the country to help optimize performance through habit formation, exercise programming, and mindset coaching.

Outside of the performance space, Joe is determined to share his story of sight loss, struggle, faith, and positive perspective through writing, speaking, and various forms of media. He actively writes for his blog, cultivates a weekly email newsletter focused on personal improvement, and uses speaking engagements to share his story and outlook on life.

Beyond this book and below every title, Joe defines himself as a human being with the goal of leaving this world better than he found it in every way possible.

Connect with Joe:
Blog: https://joerinaldi.blog/
Twitter: https://twitter.com/joearinaldi
Instagram: https://www.instagram.com/joearinaldi
Newsletter: https://www.patreon.com/joerinaldi
YouTube: https://www.youtube.com/channel/UCy7YJ4Vhk7Ph74b LIFBy-rA

Chapter 3

IT DOES END
BY DARCI SMITH

The blinding glare of the lights at night, the audience screaming wildly before every game, having something to prove out on the field, and killing myself for my teammates...

It is all gone. In a matter of seconds, the moment I have been waiting for, pushing my body to the limit, has been taken away from me. Staying positive in this shocking moment would be the best course of action, but all I can do is wrack my brain with what-ifs.

I know this had to happen for a reason, but right now I can't find it, nor do I think I ever will. Soccer was the one thing that let me escape. When I stepped on the field, I felt as if nothing else mattered. A sense of calm came over me, telling me I was where I was meant to be. The problems at home, the self-confidence, the pain, all of it disappeared. For those ninety minutes, the only thing on my mind was winning.

How do I escape these feelings for the next year? I can't just step on the field. My coping mechanism is gone. I have nothing else that made me feel as free, confident, and happy as this sport has. I know I will get through it, but why did it have to happen now? I was ready to move on with my life, and now I am at a standstill. My playing time at South Carolina State University is over. My heart and soul will still be on this team. Soccer is the reason I attended college in the first place, and it will always be a part of me.

Conference, here we come. I'll be on the sideline with my foot as close to the boundary line as possible.

I wrote the passage above in 2012, which was supposed to be *the year*. I was finally a senior, my soccer team was at the top of our game, and I was going to help us win it all. Unfortunately, that wasn't the case. That summer, while playing in a semiprofessional soccer league, I tore my left anterior cruciate ligament (ACL). I still have a hard time describing the thoughts that went through my head when I heard the unmistakable *pop* in my left knee.

As the pain radiated through my leg, I hit the ground and rolled onto my back, grabbing at my injury in shock.

Stop being a baby, I thought. *You're fine!* It was the typical athlete reaction. However, when I stood up and tried to put pressure on my leg, I knew I was not fine. I knew in my gut that it was bad, and there was a good chance I was not going to be playing soccer during my senior year of college.

The day after my surgery, I remember lying on my parents' couch and thinking that I needed to get my thoughts out on paper. It was a strange feeling because I had never been the journaling type. I wasn't one to express my feelings, and I never told people when something was wrong. Heck, I can't even remember a single time when I truly felt vulnerable in college. Prior to my surgery, I was stubborn and willful. I never thought *I* would be the one to get hurt.

However, I quickly realized this was not going to be a simple recovery. I would not be hopping back on the field, the poster child of a miracle comeback. I decided I needed to change my typical stubborn ways, and make sure I was taking the actions necessary to retain my mental toughness. I would not be able to play my sport or go on a run to clear my head and regain focus. Instead, I needed to find another outlet, and that turned out to be writing.

Now, as I read the words that I wrote in that vulnerable moment, I am proud of myself. I appreciate that knee injury rather than mad at it. I am not upset that I missed my senior year, or that I was injured. Instead, I feel changed. I can now recognize how pivotal this moment was. Since that day, journaling has become a regular practice for me. I am not going to tell you that I journal every day or every week for that matter, but I have made a habit of writing out my thoughts.

Whether they're positive, negative, creative, or just flat-out weird, I put them all down on paper. This practice helps me sleep better, releases negative energy, and fuels my creativity. Michael J. Breus, a clinical psychologist, and sleep specialist says in *Psychology Today*, "Writing your thoughts in a journal can be a very effective way of processing your feelings. Not only that, but journaling can help you recognize unproductive or negative thoughts and behaviors, and help you respond to these behaviors in a more constructive way. And when you can handle life's stresses in a positive way, it's much easier to sleep well at night."

If you're anything like me, then your brain is probably going a mile a minute, especially right when you want to go to sleep. To help avoid those endless thoughts and sleepless nights, keep a pen and paper next to your bed. Jot some of it down. Or, if you're going to be on your phone before bed anyway, pull up the notepad and start to type.

It took getting injured for me to face the reality that competitive athletics do come to an end. We try to push the fact out of our minds, but it's true. Your athletic career has an expiration date. However, your identity as an athlete doesn't have to perish along with it. Up until I was physically forced to stop playing soccer, it was the only thing I thought about.

I would think about ways I could be a better player and teammate, and I would even dream up scenarios or situations in my head where I could change the trajectory of a game. It consumed me, and I loved it! When soccer was no longer my main priority, I didn't know how to replace it. What else could fuel me the way competitive soccer did? It took me a very long time to figure this out.

I tried playing in recreational leagues, I tried other sports, I even tried watching soccer instead, which lasted all of one day, because I *hate* spectating. Watching the action on the field never invigorated me like being the one on the field did. I kept chasing that specific passion I felt when I played, but it never came. It took about a year of searching until I finally realized that I needed to look at the situation differently. Why was I trying to replicate what soccer added to my life? My time of being a competitive college athlete was over, and that was okay. I realized I needed to channel my energy into something new. But what would that be?

College had been a game-changer for me. It was my first big opportunity to step out of my normal routine. I graduated high school at seventeen years old, and only a couple of months after, I packed up my belongings, left California, and drove across the country to start my college career. I received a full-ride scholarship to attend South Carolina State University and play on the women's soccer team. I didn't know a single person there, but I was ready to expand my horizons and grow as an individual.

I had lived in the same house my entire life, I had a core group of friends, and I was known in my hometown as Darci the "athletic one." There was nothing wrong with that title; in fact, I always embraced it. But I never realized the true depth of my character until I put myself into a new environment, and I am so grateful that I did.

After graduating college, I decided I wasn't done learning. Well, truthfully I had no idea what I wanted to do with my life yet, so I figured I'd just keep going to school. I moved back to my home state and completed my MBA at California State University, in Los Angeles. The connections I built through that graduate program are what propelled my adult life. I cannot emphasize enough how much networking during this time changed my life.

In undergrad, I always stuck to my athletic circle. I did everything with my soccer team. Our teachers and mentors would tell us all the time to network, but I mostly just brushed it off. It wasn't until graduate school when I truly recognized the power of connecting with other like-minded people. This action of putting yourself out there is scary, and the concept of meeting strangers and engaging in conversation to build rapport is terrifying! I found that networking is a lot like cold calling, but in person, talk about awful.

Am I convincing you to go mingle and collaborate with strangers yet? Probably not. Well, let me just say, I have had job opportunities, business ventures, and lifelong friendships come out of this graduate program and the connections I made there, and it was all because I pushed myself to attend events and meet new people outside of my athletic circle. If you haven't joined a club, a community program, or attended a networking event yet, this is your sign!

After all the schoolwork, class projects, athletics, and networking, I landed my first job in the corporate world, but I quickly realized that something wasn't right. I was missing a part of *me*. I convinced myself it was the job, that it wasn't right for me, and I left. But now I have come to see that it wasn't my work that was the problem.

I was missing my athletic mindset. I had let it die. I didn't carry my purpose into everything I was doing, my drive to be better and win at anything I tried, and therefore, I felt empty. It took me a while to figure it out, but you don't need to go through the same thing.

After spending two years in corporate America, where I worked with a large staff of over a hundred people and sold industrial products to strangers, I decided I wanted to expand my skillset. Two things I knew for sure: I loved talking to people, and I loved making connections. So, I used my experience in sales and landed a job as an agency recruiter.

Agency recruiting meant that I was able to work with hundreds of different hiring managers across multiple industries. I worked with over forty companies in the US and got to learn the ins and outs of what hiring teams were looking for in candidates. My role in recruiting was all about meeting new people and figuring out the best way to sell their personalities, skills, and strengths to these companies.

Throughout my four years as a recruiter, I not only helped introduce candidates to jobs, but also walked the applicants through the entire job search process. I revamped countless resumes, met with candidates over zoom to do in-depth interview preparation, and I acted as a soundboard for anyone who needed career advice. I thoroughly loved seeing people excel in their careers.

After gaining knowledge and expertise in career mentorship, I decided that I wanted to help more people. In recruiting I was limited to working with candidates who were the right fit for jobs I was hiring for. Becoming an online career coach was an opportunity to reach a larger audience. I dove headfirst into social media, created a website, and started marketing my career services.

I am now a career coach, and I get to help people navigate tough career decisions. I get to see people have fun as they prepare for interviews and see the joy on their faces when they negotiate their offer for higher pay. I can't tell you where I will be in the next five to ten years, but what I know for sure is that I am going to be doing something that brings joy into people's lives.

I picked up new passions, I worked on vulnerability, and I am now at a place where I am happy and feel filled with a desire for life.

In order to realize my version of being a Forever Athlete, I had to recognize that "Darci the soccer player" was no longer, but "Darci the athlete" was forever. I had to do a lot of self-reflecting. I engaged in deep conversations and built connections with people outside my sports bubble. I am so proud of the person I am today. I am unique, confident, and curious, and I have owned who I am.

I am the person at the party who won't shut up. I am the girl playing wingman for a stranger I just met at the bar. I am the one who always goes a little over the top if that's what it takes to get a good story. I am the friend you call for no reason at all.

Sometimes I pretend I am on a reality tv show and narrate my day as if there's a camera following me. I am an animal lover. I am so many things beyond being an athlete. It is not the only interesting thing about me, nor the only thing worth telling others. I know my life's purpose. It is so simple but so perfect. My life's purpose is to create fun and happiness for the people around me.

Seeing other people smile, dance, celebrate, and enjoy life truly fuels me. I know that I was put on this planet to help others see the joy in life. This purpose is what drove me to contribute to this book. Ever since I discovered what my true purpose is, I feel like have I unlocked the secret to happy living: if I have something to share, I jump on the opportunity to do so. It is my wish that you, too, will be able to unlock your life's purpose and live in a way that fulfills you and allows you to utilize the unique mindset that can only come from being a Forever Athlete.

But, what does it *mean* to be a Forever Athlete? Have you ever had your friends tell you, "You're too competitive," or "It's just a game"?

I know I have, and it always used to frustrate me. No matter how hard I tried to turn off that competitive part of me, it always came out. Whether it was a game of cards, a Christmas gift exchange, or a friendly round of beer pong, I always had to win. I would try so hard to play it cool or pretend I didn't care, but that's not who I am.

I am competitive in everything I do; that's who I am to my core. These days, I embrace it. I love that my competitive nature follows me everywhere I go. It is a simple reminder that the athlete in me will never die. As I move throughout my daily life, I know that being a Forever Athlete is not only about wanting to win. It is also about continuously pushing the envelope, always learning, challenging myself, and being there for my team.

I want to share with you some steps I took to find new passions. If you want to embrace your inner Forever Athlete as well, you need to gain a better understanding of what you want your life to look like beyond your athletic career. Grab a pen and paper, or your phone, and follow these steps to get started:

Step 1: Set a timer for thirty seconds. Write down the top three goals in your life right now. Do these goals represent a bigger ambition? Do these goals surprise you? Are they attainable?

Step 2: Set your timer for sixty seconds this time. If you only had three months to live, how would your top three goals change? What would they be instead? Are they attainable?

Think about your answers in step one compared to your answers now. Why are they different? Are you taking active steps toward any of these goals right now? If not, let's change that. By changing your answers, you have just revealed to yourself what you *truly* want. If you only had a short amount of time left on this earth, these are the things you would like to accomplish.

Step 3: If you had all the money and resources in the world, what would you be doing? There is no fear of failing and there are no limits. You can do anything you want. So, what would you want to accomplish if there was nothing holding you back?

Step 4: Review. Go back and read through all your answers. Is there a common theme? Do you want to travel, learn new things, or overcome challenges? Do your answers reflect a desire to be surrounded by other people, or do you want to be on your own? Find the common denominator in your goals and wishes.

If you can identify this theme, you can determine the next steps in pushing toward these goals using your athletic mindset. In turn, you will know how to embrace your version of a Forever Athlete. Heads up, it's not the same for every athlete, and it will take an immense amount of personal growth on your part to get there.

Growth comes from pushing through the uncomfortable parts of life. I have never heard anyone say, "Man, I am really grateful I went through that easy time in my life. It really made me grow."

We must embrace the struggle, and trust that we will come out the other side stronger than we were before. These opportunities for growth show up in many different forms. Whether it's a career change, a new friend group, or overcoming a mental or physical hurdle, you will find plenty of moments to embrace the challenges that lead to development.

For me, being uncomfortable meant finding my true identity. Because I had identified solely as an athlete for so long, I had no idea what it meant to identify as Darci. I set out to answer some important questions about myself.

Who was I without sports? Who was I to other people? How was I adding to society? After reflecting, I was able to restructure my identity. I was still a passionate and competitive person at heart. I was someone people relied on and turned to in times of need. I was the kind of person who joined clubs and signed up for volunteer work. I became more involved in my community.

Once I was able to answer these questions, I knew how to fully embrace the feeling of being uncomfortable. Finding the answers to the hard questions, the ones that plague you and keep you up at night is what is necessary to achieve more and grow beyond your limitations.

I am sure you have heard the saying, "You have to celebrate the small wins." Athletes have many up and downs, so how do we stay grounded on this rollercoaster? By celebrating minor achievements. I heard this advice countless times during my athletic career, but as you can probably guess, I never took it to heart.

I never celebrated anything small. It was all or nothing, zero to one hundred, all of the time. I didn't care if I played well, learned a new skill, or completed a project; if it didn't result in a win, it was not worth celebrating. It took me years to realize how important this really is. It's the small victories that motivate you to push until you hit the big one.

Let's practice this. Instead of focusing only on the end goal, think about the ways you can win along the way.

Let's say my goal is to lose fifteen pounds. Instead of simply writing that down and leaving it there, I will come up with five small, attainable steps to help me reach that goal. In order to lose fifteen pounds, I will:

1. Grocery shop once a week.
2. Meal prep on Sundays and Wednesdays.

3. Take a progress photo once a week.
4. Weigh myself every morning.
5. Work out for at least forty-five minutes per day, six days of the week.

Now, you try. Think of a goal you would like to achieve and come up with five, small steps you can take to get there.

Next, write down the milestones you will celebrate during the journey to your overall goal. This is the step I was always missing. I knew my goal, I knew the steps I had to take to get there, but I never wrote down the moments along the way that needed recognition. On my way to losing fifteen pounds, I will celebrate:

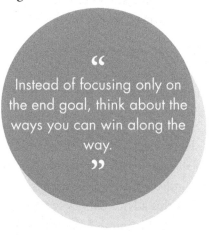

" Instead of focusing only on the end goal, think about the ways you can win along the way. "

1. The first five pounds lost.
2. Three weeks of clean eating and sticking to the meal prep.
3. Hitting a PR (personal record) in the gym.
4. Meditate every day for ten days in a row.

So, what milestones will you celebrate along the way to your goal? Write them down.

The last step in this process is to identify *how* you will celebrate each of these small wins. You must put action to the celebration to make it feel real and worth striving toward. Make each small celebration something to look forward to and keep you motivated. For example, when I lose the first five pounds I will buy myself a new pair of workout shorts. After I complete ten days of meditation, I will reward myself by booking a massage.

All the milestones you have laid out to reach your goal are important. If you celebrate the small wins along the way, you are more likely to keep pushing yourself all the way to your ultimate goal.

Have you put real thought into what you want your life to look like post-sports? Have you identified as an athlete for so long that you're not sure how to break out of that mindset? Are you struggling to transition your athlete's mindset into regular life?

As athletes, we spend so much of our life being told what to do and how to do it. Now, it's your turn to take control. You're the coach, and your life is the game. How are you going to capture that win?

ABOUT DARCI

Darci Smith was born and raised in Bakersfield, California, where she spent her early years dedicated to becoming a top-performing athlete. At seventeen years old, she moved across the country to attend South Carolina State University and accomplish her childhood dream of playing D1 college soccer. When that dream was complete, it was time to find a new purpose.

Darci describes herself as a free-spirited, social, and unique person with a desire to constantly challenge herself. She completed her MBA at California State University Los Angeles, and after spending time in the corporate world, she has now pivoted her skills and desire to help others into her role as a career coach. She has helped thousands of recent graduates and seasoned business professionals find their purpose and crush their career goals.

She loves pushing the envelope and helping others step outside of their comfort zones. When Darci is not working, she can almost always be found at the dog park, a winery, or on the pickleball courts. Regardless of where she is or what she is doing, Darci will always be the most competitive person in the room. Connect with Darci on Instagram at @careercoachdarci.

Chapter 4

LIVING BEYOND THE LABEL, WITHOUT BORDERS
BY DR. MATT WIEST

From an early age, I deeply connected my identity to sports. It was who I was, the focus of most conversations, and the only lens through which I felt my peers saw me. I took pride in wearing the track suit with the big crest on my chest while I strutted through the hallways at school. My status as an athlete was always the first thing I introduced myself with, right after my name.

I would say, "Hi, I am Matt. I am a hockey player from southern Alberta."

Sometimes it would be, "Hi, I am Matt. I played rugby during grad school."

Or, "Hi, I am Matt. I am on the hockey team on campus."

Before where I was from, what I was studying, or my professional career, I was an athlete. I recognized this as my sense of worth and purpose, but I knew that a professional career in hockey or rugby was not in the cards for me. So, I began seeking out career opportunities that would align with being an athlete. What could I do that would allow me to maintain this identity? If that was who I was, what did a future look like for someone like me?

My story highlights this journey and brings to light the transition in perspective on what being an athlete has meant to me, how it has impacted the growth of my business, and how this shows up in my life today as an entrepreneur, a leader, and a father.

When I was seventeen, I moved from my hometown in Southern Alberta, Canada to Vancouver to play junior hockey. Fresh out of high school and ready to take on this new journey, I was excited to experience a new city, new people, and new opportunities. I played in the BCHL for four years, on three different teams, and had a great time. I cultivated incredible lifelong friendships, made some mistakes along the way, and grew a lot as a young adult. Those four years also acted as buffer time to figure out what I wanted to do in my next chapter of life.

In my spare time (which, looking back, there was a lot of), I was sniffing out career options to pursue. During this period, I suffered from multiple injuries and felt like my physical health was taking a beating. We were on the ice almost every day; rehab and recovery quickly became a necessity in order to keep up with the demands of the sport.

Because of this, I was inspired to get involved in a career that would help address the physical rehabilitation side of sports. I knew I wanted to be adjacent to the world of athletics and somewhere in healthcare, but I wasn't sure about which route I wanted to take.

I shadowed a few dentists, athletic therapists, and sports medicine physicians, but nothing felt quite right. I was looking for something that had the potential for a lot of autonomy, everything I had seen up to that point felt like plugging into a cookie-cutter system, and I knew that wasn't what I was looking for.

Eventually, I connected with our team trainer who was just entering into chiropractic school at the time, and he piqued my interest in looking further into what it meant to be involved in that field. I loved what chiropractic had to offer: a large scope of practice, working one-on-one with people, the opportunity to work with athletes, and most importantly to me, the freedom to get creative in the way I helped my future patients find solutions to their problems.

After a few positive experiences rehabbing an injury of my own with a chiropractor, I knew this was the path I wanted to take. This decision began my journey into the next chapter of my life and gave me what I felt was a broader sense of identity. I was no longer only focused on hockey. I had a career to pursue, a next chapter to write. Little did I know how much of an impact my experience as an athlete would have on how I showed up as a clinician.

After junior hockey, I played four years of college hockey in Superior, Wisconsin, while studying exercise science. During this period of time, I was focused on preparation for my career; I busied myself with prerequisite courses, dreaming up business plans, and connecting with others in the profession. I was still excited about the sport and competing, but it was fun building this new side of me, fueling another newfound passion outside of hockey.

Once my senior year began to wind down, I felt a mixed bag of emotions. I was sad that my participation in the sport I had invested my entire life into was coming to a close but also appreciative for all that it had brought into my life. Most of all, I was excited about what was to come. Looking back at this pivotal time makes me even more grateful that I was in a place where my identity was broadening.

I have so many friends and old teammates who struggled in varying degrees with this transition as it can be very lonely.

Who am I now that I am no longer competitively participating in my sport? What am I doing now that my identity is shifting? Where am I headed?

These questions are ones that a lot of my former teammates have asked themselves as they closed this chapter and moved on to the next.

Sometimes, the answers to these questions can leave you feeling lost and alone. I don't know if I realized it at the time, but looking back, these thoughts were definitely going through my head even though I had a plan for what was next. I still felt a sense of emptiness, and my mental wellbeing was suffering as I treaded into uncertainty. It was as though a part of me was being left behind as I embarked on a new adventure.

Finally, the time came for me to begin my doctorate program at Palmer College of Chiropractic in Davenport, Iowa. I was coming right off officially wrapping up my hockey career and found myself in a new city once again, this time without my thirty automatic new best friends waiting for me at training camp. The program I was in was intense, but I found myself using skills I gained from hockey to dive in headfirst. Time management, dedication, and social connection all came into play.

For the first time in my life, I was going to have to meet people on my own. I was in uncharted territory. I knew it was important for me to create a network of people I could count on. Social wellbeing is at the epicenter of everything for me, and I needed a support system in place to have any chance at survival.

I was used to making friends with people who were similar to me—attracted to the same things, with similar backgrounds, and similar life paths. Without that common interest (hockey), I was making friends from diverse backgrounds—some with athletic backgrounds, others without, some from fraternities, and others from international undergraduate programs. I was forced to move beyond the label of "I am a hockey player," and tap into deeper and broader interests to cultivate connections.

In grad school I met new faces with interesting perspectives, and, in many ways, I was pushed out of my comfort zone socially for the first time. About three months in, I was feeling an itch to compete. I missed hockey and how it pushed me physically and mentally.

To a degree, the grad program I was in did this; the curriculum was challenging, but it felt like I was in it alone. Even though I had made plenty of friends and felt like I had support, we were all working on our own aspirations, not together toward a team goal.

I felt like I needed an outlet for this part of my soul, one that allowed me to work with others on a common mission. Around the same time, I was approached to play rugby for a local team and ended up playing for the next four years.

As grad school was coming to a close, I began to feel the pressure to figure out who I was in this next chapter: "Matt the clinician." I had plenty of ideas for what I thought that was going to look like. I knew I eventually wanted to open my own practice, but I wasn't feeling quite ready to take the plunge into entrepreneurship. Because of my background in sports, I was eager to work with athletes. It was what I knew, and it was what made sense.

I decided to look for a clinic that embodied the work culture I was looking for. It was important for me to work with a clinical team, one that valued physical activity and educating their patients. I was searching for an environment where I could work on my clinical skills and be surrounded by like-minded people working toward a common mission for a few years before venturing out on my own.

Time was ticking down, and a few months before graduation, my wife and I decided to make the move to Minneapolis, Minnesota, where I found a great opportunity at a sports rehab clinic to start my career as Dr. Matt Wiest.

Moving to the Land of 10,000 Lakes was an exciting time. I was in a new city, jumping into a new career, and freshly married with a little one on the way—so much change in such a condensed amount of time! The clinic that I found was exactly what I expected; the staff was my new team. We worked hard together, pushed each other, and worked with a ton of athletes from high school level to professional. I had landed my perfect gig.

I worked hard and studied harder, and it turned out graduation was just the beginning. I didn't have much time or energy for anything outside of work, but that's how it is supposed to be, right? Success means always being on the grind ... or, at least, that's what I told myself.

But as time went on, I started to feel burned out, frustrated and lost. The framework was great, but something was missing for me. About two years in, I decided it was time to create some change.

I still didn't know if I was ready to start my own business, but I did know that, if I didn't change something, I might not be cut out for the industry much longer. I don't think I realized it at the moment, but a big contributor to me hitting this low point was the fact that I was living under the mask of whom I thought I needed to be as a professional.

As a clinician, I needed to dress a certain way, look polished, and know my shit all the time. I needed to have all the answers to "fix" people so they could get back on the ice/field/court.

I was so blinded by wanting to work with what my definition of an athlete was that I was missing the evolved reason I wanted to do this work—the true *why* behind what I wanted to do in the industry and the change I wanted to be part of in healthcare. I was no longer the nineteen-year-old boy trying to find ways to recover from a banged-up body to get back on the ice. I had developed a grander perspective on what it meant to me to be an athlete and to be healthy.

I searched for opportunities to provide space for my community to improve not only their physical health but also their mental and social health. It was important to me to not only provide them the tools to rehab their physical ailments but to validate their mental struggles and create a community around self-improvement. I wanted to do it by building social connections with a wide variety of individuals.

Gyms can do it. Sports teams can do it. Why couldn't / shouldn't your clinical provider strive to offer the same? I had a lot of work to do, but I was determined to make moves and do some deep digging. I was on a mission to better understand how I could create a culture that promoted mental, physical, and social wellbeing in a health care setting.

After about six months of taking my foot off the gas and refocusing my vision, I was ready to take the leap and jump into starting my own business. In March of 2017, The Center of Movement was born—a brand focused on empowering and educating our communities to discover sustainable solutions to support mental, physical, and social wellbeing. This new adventure was different.

I was channeling the Forever Athlete inside me in a new, adapted way. I was no longer focused on working with the athlete as an ideal patient; I was more interested in creating a culture where taking responsibility for our mental, physical, and social wellbeing is not only accepted but celebrated.

Whether you are a pro athlete or a weekend warrior, it is our duty to take control of our health in this way , for ourselves and for the people around us. Our brand taps into that feeling I had in grad school, that feeling of working hard alone and how isolating that can be and brings this to the wellbeing space. Nobody wants to recover from an injury alone or go through everyday stresses that come with pain alone. We are all in it together.

This might seem out of the box for a chiropractor, but my experiences as an athlete have shown me how these three areas of health are critical in navigating through life. My experiences as a clinician have shown me just how tightly intertwined these areas are with one another. I still work with athletes all day, every day, but my definition of "athlete" has evolved.

It no longer only includes the pro who is out on the ice thirteen months out of the year. It's the junior varsity hockey player trying to find his way through the high school bullies. It's the new mom working on connecting with others and prioritizing her wellbeing.

It might be the college athlete recovering from a back injury in his senior year or the stressed-out CEO finding ways to improve her mental health. My definition includes anyone who is working hard and seeking out sustainable solutions for their health. We are stronger together.

I know this wasn't the case for many. Most of my peers were chasing the dream, the next level, the professional career. Not me. Did I love hockey?

Absolutely. But I was there for the community, the brotherhood, and the camaraderie, and it has wholly influenced my business vision and purpose. Society likes to make you think that you need to live within boxes.

"I am an athlete."
"I am a chiropractor."

These are just labels.

> "Whether you are a pro athlete or a weekend warrior, it is our duty to take control of our health in this way, for ourselves and for the people around us."

They can exist as a part of who you are, but they can challenge your identity when you start to own them as your only truth. These labels are not deep-rooted characteristics or personality traits. They are not interpersonal skills or developed perspectives on life as we know it, and they do not define *who* you are, and *how* you show up.

I have learned over the years that true growth comes from being agile and accepting that labels change, but that doesn't mean you need to be left behind with these changes. You are an adaptable creature who is ever-evolving based on the life experiences you have had. Each experience allows you a fresh perspective and more clarity. You will always be an athlete. Nothing is going to change that. But a better question to ask yourself might be, "What makes me an athlete?" or "How has being an athlete shaped who I am today?"

When you look at your life and the relationships you've built, the outlook you've adopted, the grand vision you have—how has being a Forever Athlete shaped those things for you?

For me, it has provided the necessary tools to build community. It has created a standard for my social wellbeing, sharpened communication skills, and taught me the importance of adapting. Most importantly, my identity as a Forever Athlete has given me the confidence to live beyond the label, without borders.

ABOUT DR. MATT

Dr. Matt Wiest grew up in Enchant, Alberta, Canada, a small farming community just east of the Rocky Mountains. After high school, Matt spent three years in Vancouver playing junior hockey. He then moved to Wisconsin to play college hockey at the University of Wisconsin—Superior where he earned his Bachelor of Exercise Science in Wellness and Fitness Management.

Matt continued his education in Davenport, Iowa at Palmer College of Chiropractic, where he earned his Doctorate of Chiropractic (D.C.) degree. It was through his experience in athletics that Matt's passion for human optimization grew.

Through personal experience, as well as witnessing firsthand numerous teammates seeking solutions where they could take matters into their own hands, Matt knew that this was the direction he was meant to go with his clinical career and small business.

Matt is the owner and operator of The Center of Movement in the Twin Cities, Minnesota. It is a group focused on educating and empowering their communities to discover sustainable solutions to support their physical, mental, and social wellbeing.

In his free time, Matt enjoys hockey, rugby, hiking, yoga, connecting with interesting people, hearing their stories, and spending time with his wife, Britny, and their daughters, Nara and Georgia.

Chapter 5

ONE OF THE NINETY8PERCENT

BY DEPHANIE ADEYEMI

According to the NCAA, only two percent of collegiate athletes go pro. So, what happens to the other ninety-eight percent? Well, I'm a part of the ninety-eight percent, and I'd like to share a bit of my story with you.

In 2008, I sat on the couch in my parents' living room, eyes glued to the television, watching Usain Bolt run the greatest 100/200m race at the time. I was mesmerized by the thousands of people who filled the stadium and the caliber of competition from all over the world representing their country.

Then there was Allyson Felix. I was captivated by the way she ran the 200m. She stood only five feet, six inches tall, but the length of her stride made it seem as if she was six feet tall. She covered a lot of ground in so little time. I was enthralled by the way she hugged the turn and picked up speed along the straight without looking exhausted. Although she came in second place, I knew I wanted to model my race after her.

It was on that day I decided to be one of the greatest track athletes to set foot on this earth. I wanted to stand alongside other Olympians such as Usain Bolt, Allyson Felix, Flo Jo, Lolo Jones, Jai Richardson, Tyson Gay, Muna Lee, Michael Johnson, and Carl Lewis.

The idea of wearing red, white, and blue, of the USA across my chest, and my last name, "Adeyemi," on my bib, represented the ultimate American dream to me. My parents, both Nigerian immigrants, spent their lives striving to achieve the American dream. They worked hard every day to provide a life for us that was better than the childhood they had. They stressed the importance of education because they knew it was critical to success in America.

My dad, Tony, is no stranger to education, discipline, and hard work, which he brought home with him every day. Standing at a little over six feet, with a briefcase in hand, he would bring his cell phone to his ear and say welcomingly, "Moshi Moshi." He obtained his master's in electrical engineering in Japan, where he became fluent in Japanese. The pursuit of education was of the utmost importance to him, and he married a woman who equally valued it.

My mom, Lola, is more on the creative side. She was a dancer, an actress, and a TV news anchor. She even owned her own dance studio in Nigeria. Her first degree is in theater arts. Then, after she had my sister, she went back to school for nursing, and ultimately earned two degrees. It was never lost on me that my mom raised two kids, was a full-time student, kept a clean house, put food on the table, and made sure we were well-dressed every day for school. She's a superhero, my superhero.

Being a first-generation Nigerian-American was not easy. As a young girl in the first grade, my days were spent scribbling my times tables and being reminded I could not succeed in America without my education.

After finishing my homework for the evening, I would have to journal a one-page summary detailing the events of my day. My dad titled the entries "My Days."

"Did you write your *My Day* today?" he would ask. "Let me see. I hope you didn't miss a day, or else no TV."

My parents kept me disciplined since I was five years old. At around ten, I found my passion for athletics. Although education remained number one in my house, my parents allowed me to dabble in sports.

Figure skating, tennis, soccer, ballet, basketball, you name it, I did it. As Nigerian immigrants, little did my parents and I know that another way to free education in America, apart from a high GPA, was through sports.

In my freshman year of high school, I decided to try out for the track team. It was a semi-warm day in January of 2009, and everyone seemed to have known each other prior to tryouts. Nonetheless, I was ready to prove I had the speed to be on the team.

"Get on the line! You. You! You with the blue shorts," Coach yelled.

"On my whistle, go. Ready. Set." The whistle blew.

I whispered to myself, "Deph, pick up your feet, lift your knees, pump your arms."

Before I knew it, the 100m was over, and I had strained my hamstring. I had never known a pain like that before. It was the inaugural track injury, the first I ever had, and it wouldn't be the last.

Despite the injuries that plagued my entire high school career, I won nearly every race I ran. I started out in the 100, 200, and any relay of my choice to help my team score points and increase training endurance for bigger meets.

I was a decent high jumper out of middle school but had to forgo field events entirely by sophomore year. I realized that the stress of an additional event, on top of three races, caused severe shin splints. So, I focused only on running.

The drive to excel in school, I brought to the track. I became the leading track athlete, not only at my school, but within the district and region, and I was one of the top sprinters in the state. After only starting track at thirteen years old, I realized I was very good at it, and I fell in love with competing.

Although my grades didn't impress my dad when people came to him and asked, "Are you Dephanie's dad?"

It lit up his whole world. At this point, all I had to do was keep up decent grades and keep winning on the track. Track and field brought me so much joy, and I loved that my success made my parents proud. By the end of my high school career, I was a five-time state finalist, eleven-time regional qualifier and finalist, and had won several district championship races. Meanwhile, I was the school record holder in the 100m, 200m, 4x100m relay, and 4x200m relay. Somehow, everyone knew me by "Track Star," or by my infamous Twitter handle, @ purplesprinter. It was wild!

On signing day, every one of my family members and friends had on a blue shirt with gold letters that spelled out "UCLA" on their chest. It was one of the proudest moments of our lives. Not only was I going to attend one of the greatest universities in the world, but I had received a full-ride scholarship. My family had no clue this was a possibility coming from Nigeria, and yet we were blessed far beyond our imagination.

With high school graduation in June of 2012, I had set goals for what I expected out of college. I wanted only three things to come out of my college experience going into the 2016 Olympic year: a civil engineering degree, to make the qualifying time for the Olympic trials, and a secure job after graduation.

Well, none of those things happened. Not even close. Christmas break, of my freshman year, I was straining to walk one foot in front of the other.

"Coach, I'm in so much pain. I can barely stand on my feet anymore," I said.

I admired my coach, Jeannette Bolden. She was an Olympic gold medalist and a big reason why I had chosen to come to UCLA. Concern entered her voice as she told me to stop training and immediately schedule an x-ray and MRI upon my return to campus.

There was a stigma against athletes with shin splints.

"You're weak," my teammates would say. "It's not that bad. Just tape them. Use ice. They'll go away."

With every step I took, it felt like needles protruding my bones, and knots gathered in every section of the bottom of my feet. It was hard to walk or gently set my feet on the floor simply getting out of bed.

I'd been pushing through the pain during practice for months, taping my shins under my leggings and using Biofreeze to numb the pain so I could train with the team. I felt that, if I exposed my pain, I could potentially lose my scholarship and disappoint everyone who had been following my track career.

When the MRI showed a grade-four stress reaction in both of my shins, it didn't feel like a disappointment but more of a setback.

Maybe you've heard the saying, "A minor setback is a setup for a major comeback." I had so much faith that I would be able to return to the sport within a couple of weeks.

Inevitably, I had to redshirt my freshman year. To "redshirt" is to forgo competing in a season, but with the ability to later compete an extra year at school. Although I kept my disappointment and sadness to myself, it reflected in my schoolwork and relationships. I don't think we understand how much we manifest outwardly what we are feeling inside. I started to fail my quizzes, exams, and labs.

Even though I studied for hours every day, attended tutoring sessions, and sat in for office hours, I struggled in every subject related to math and science.

I started to believe the lie that I wasn't smart enough for the major, and I wasn't sure if I would make it out of there with a degree. I constantly replayed my dad's words in my head:

"Dephanie, without math, you can do nothing."

At that point, I felt like a disappointment to my parents.

"Mom, I think I want to change my major."

I had already switched from engineering to biology, and then to psychobiology. I was having a hard time finding my passion in school and aiming for decent grades. My parents were baffled at the fact that I had changed my major three times by my sophomore year in college.

"Dephanie, this is not how the real world works. You need to pick a major and stick with it. Pick a major that will give you a job that will last the test of time."

I didn't know how to tell them I was on academic probation for the second time in three-quarters, and my GPA wasn't high enough to continue the major anymore. Because I couldn't share the truth, and every conversation with my parents ended in tears, I stopped calling them. That was the beginning of isolation. I started spending less time with teammates and friends.

I put all my energy into studying, rehab, and meeting my professors during their office hours, but still, nothing improved.

Am I getting dumber? Am I smart enough to be at UCLA? Should I transfer?

I experienced so much doubt in my intelligence, which is what got me into UCLA in the first place.

I failed to understand that emotions can affect judgment and decision-making. Regardless of how much I tried to keep my cool, anxiety, depression, disappointment, and shame affected all my actions, whether it was doing poorly at exams, snapping back in conversations, or choosing solitude instead of socializing.

By sophomore year, I returned to the track, nearly healthy with no shin pain, and finally able to be around teammates again. Sadly, within a month of intense training, my shins began to hurt again. I began to question the legitimacy of my scholarship.

I remember talking to my best friend.

"Dang, we have a new coach who didn't recruit me. I had to redshirt my freshman year. How am I supposed to keep my scholarship if I have to deal with another injury when I didn't even compete last year?" I asked.

The solution? Deal with it.

I told myself there was too much riding on my athletic performance. I couldn't afford UCLA as an out-of-state student. I couldn't imagine losing my scholarship, moving back to Texas, and having to answer questions from people who'd never understand the challenges I had endured and failed to overcome. I believed more lies: that there was no strength in failure, and that there was no strength in admitting depression, anxiety, and shame.

I realize now that I never showed myself any grace or leniency in my circumstance. I was only harder on myself. My grades were still below average. I couldn't find the energy to connect with friends. My depression was so deep, and I had no clue I was even in it because even on my most painful days, I still had a smile on my face.

Strength. Discipline. Hard work. Education. These are the words I repeated daily to push through the pain and self-doubt. If my parents could come from Africa and make something out of nothing, then how could I, with all this opportunity in front of me, do better for myself?

What I thought would be the last race of the season ended up being the last race of my collegiate career. At the 2014 NCAA Regional Championships, leading my team out of the blocks in the 4x100 meter relay, I ran my leg as if my life depended on it. Which it did because your scholarship isn't guaranteed year after year.

Hobbling off the track, I was elated to finally end the season and get the rest I needed. I was worn out and stressed from intense science courses with midterms every two weeks, and after dealing with taking exams on the road, I was just thankful my grades were passing.

I took the summer to reset, retake classes, and rehab. Coach called me into the office to sign my scholarship offer for the 2014-15 year. I remember walking up the stairs in fear of reading that my scholarship would be reduced. To my amazement and relief, it still read one hundred percent.

After going into my redshirt sophomore offseason training, my shins were battered within a month. I knew it was the end of my season, and besides, I also became ineligible due to poor grades. Every night I went to bed crying in disappointment and shame.

Midway into the winter quarter, which was also the indoor season, I received a call from my coach for a one-on-one meeting. I thought they were going to kick me out of school or take my scholarship away.

"Dephanie, there comes a time when every athlete has to be honest with themselves. You were, and I believe still are, one of the best athletes in the nation, but your body has struggled to withstand the intensity of the training. You have worked hard every day to get back, and I can tell you're tired and in pain. I would like to offer you a medical retirement. You get to keep your full scholarship and just enjoy going to school."

After contemplating this for two weeks, I took the medical retirement. It was like a bag of bricks was lifted off my back. I knew I needed a change, but I couldn't make the initial decision for fear of losing everything. I didn't know what my options were, but everything started to click. Two weeks later, I expressed to my academic advisor that I wanted to change my major from biology to sociology.

"Dephanie, there's no way you can finish the sociology requirements within a year," my academic advisor warned.

I said, "Watch me."

With the same determination, discipline, and strength my parents had instilled in me, I walked out of UCLA with a degree in sociology with a focus in pre-medicine in the spring of 2016, the Olympic year.

I didn't know how to let go of track and field, because that was all I knew. *What now? What's next?* Within the Nigerian community, it is a long-running joke that our parents expect us to become one of three things: an engineer, lawyer, or doctor. But nobody's really joking.

Realistically, as long as you fall within any of those subcategories, your parents will be proud.

"What are you going to do with a sociology degree?" they asked me.

I had no clue. I was just happy to have made it out with any degree. I thought of going back to school, but with my less than 3.0 GPA, no master's program would admit me. Besides, I didn't feel worthy, smart, or capable of returning to classes and taking exams. I knew nothing except how to be excellent on the track, and even then, I had failed miserably. When I returned to Dallas, people only remembered me for track.

"Dephanie, why aren't you running in the Olympics? Don't you miss it? Are you still training?"

I thought maybe one day I'd make it back to the track, but Coach was right. The thing that brought me so much joy was causing me too much pain. I wanted everybody to shut up. How suffocating it was to be reminded of what I could no longer do. Rather than make the conscious choice to quit, my body decided for me. Ultimately, I had to get a job and get out of Dallas, but it wasn't as easy as I thought.

I had a couple of interviews with some entertainment companies but completely failed. I was unpolished in every aspect of the word.

How can I have a degree from UCLA, but I can't land a job?

I could see the weariness in my parents' eyes, wanting the best for me, but knowing I didn't set myself up with the right degree.

My dad suggested I go to a temp agency to see if I could get a job through them.

A temp agency? With a degree from UCLA?

I couldn't allow my pride to get in the way of a job.

As I pulled up to the temp agency, I wiped my tears and fixed my suit. I took the mini math, reading, and typing exams and passed with flying colors, to the agent's amazement. The agent gasped at the school on my resume and asked why I was there. I asked her the same question back, respectfully insinuating for her to mind her business. She placed me with a company to interview, and I got the job.

It was drudgery, an office job anybody could do, but I needed a paycheck. As I entered the upper floor of the building before my eyes were rows and rows of computers. Everyone clocked in and out at the same time. There was no talking, and it was always cold. I went from living one of the most active lifestyles to being reprimanded for leaving my desk too many times because I was bored.

Seven months later, another job opportunity fell into my lap, one that required a relocation to Seattle. It was in retail marketing as a project coordinator. I gladly took the position and moved out of Dallas, where I felt the walls were closing in every day. I was overjoyed to move to a new place where nobody knew my name.

I was so ready to reinvent myself and meet new people that I nearly forgot to turn around and wave goodbye to my family at airport security.

As I met new friends from different walks, I shared my interests while completely neglecting to mention that I'd run track. It was refreshing to realize people liked me for me and not because of what I could do or used to do. I noticed something so amazing about the Seattle residents: there were Black Americans, Africans, and African Americans working at Microsoft, Amazon, Zillow, Google, etc.

There was so much Black excellence around me. I had never really been exposed to people who looked like me at my age who weren't athletes. I asked myself many questions.

What school did they go to? How did they get these nice jobs? How can I find success like them?

I learned a couple of things. None of them were athletes. They were exposed to career fairs, resume writing, and interview workshops, and somehow they worked at Fortune 100 companies.

I knew that, as a collegiate athlete, I felt I had a leg up on them. Collegiate athletes experience what it's like working for a big corporation—the NCAA. We are bound by regulations and focused on delivering quality work for the university while our fate depends on our performance. We are so focused on sports and being an athlete-student, that we don't have time for networking events, or didn't know they were happening because it wasn't emphasized enough.

I vaguely remember being told to go to these events, but I hardly understood the impact of what networking events and job fairs would have on my future beyond sports.

Did I miss all these opportunities in my four years of college? Why weren't they enforced? Was I not listening hard enough?

So many questions swarmed my mind about how I, and so many others, were not where we didn't even know we could be.

I connected with a friend who had just been introduced to business management consulting, and I expressed how tired I was in retail marketing.

He said, "Deph, come to the consulting industry!"

I dismissed that. Why would they want someone with a sociology degree?

"Deph!" he exclaimed. "People here have history, political science, and sociology degrees. Don't worry about it. Send me your resume."

So, I did. It was the first time someone believed I could achieve something greater, despite what I believed were limitations. It was the first time someone took the time to pour into me. He taught me how to write my resume, spent hours practicing interview questions, and told me how to share my story as a medically retired track and field D1 athlete.

I got the interview! Five days before my interview, I got my wisdom teeth removed, but nothing was going to stop me from going. I called in sick to my job that morning, took some painkillers, and entered the company building for my three-hour interview. I sat in the clear-windowed office, facing my interviewer with pain radiating in my jaw.

"Tell me about yourself."

"My name is Dephanie Adeyemi. I'm from Dallas, Texas, raised in a Nigerian immigrant household, and I am a first-generation American. I went to college at the University of California Los Angeles, where I was recruited to run track. While balancing fifteen credits per quarter as a pre-med student, I managed to balance twenty hours a week training in my sport.

Unfortunately, I medically retired during my junior year due to a chronic shin injury. No, my time at UCLA was not the best, as I struggled to deal with my injury and succeed at school simultaneously. At the end of junior year, I switched my major to sociology and loved it. Learning about human behavior, social constructs, and how structures, architecture, and circumstances can affect human actions amazed me.

None of this was easy. I had a dream to compete at the 2016 Rio Olympics, but my dream was crushed due to my injury, and I had to find a new path forward. I believe I'm qualified for this position because of my discipline, endurance, adaptability, and resilience. Being an athlete at UCLA taught me to communicate with senior leadership, adapt to role changes, be a team player, execute perfect time management skills, and have endurance and resilience through hardship and complications.

You're probably wondering why I want this job. I want to be an example to collegiate and pro-athletes who are finding their way and preparing themselves for a world without sports.

This job is to help me build my skill set and learn what I need to learn to navigate the corporate space even with limited experience. I might not have a clear understanding of what I want to do or who I want to be, but with the knowledge, I'll gain here, I can give back to them to make their transition smoother than mine.

Despite the hardships and challenges in lieu of their achievements, their value and contribution to the world are beyond their athleticism. It comes from the lessons learned while enduring the most challenging walks in life as a collegiate or pro-athlete."

I got the job.

One thing I valued about the interview was that they wanted to get to know me as a person. I cried while I spoke because I had never talked about my experience as a student-athlete before. It wasn't as glamorous as people on the outside may think it is. From that moment on, I understood something crucial: knowing how to tell your story in an impactful way can qualify you for any job, regardless of experience.

I didn't think it was possible for someone like me, with a sociology degree and a horrible graduating GPA, to make it into a profession like consulting and excel in the workplace with a competitive salary.

Companies tend to value GPA over work experience and the candidate's personal journey that led them to apply for the job. It's critical to know how to tell an effective and compelling story that overlooks something like GPA, or the type of school you attended, especially if your academic career does not measure up to company hiring standards.

Even through my disappointments, my parents were proud of me, regardless of the expectations they had. I made a life for myself that brought a smile to my face like track and field once did. I'm grateful to the company and team who took the time to understand me as a person and develop me into the strong consultant I am.

Sharing my story may help others understand the trials and challenges that athletes go through, as well as inspire athletes and teach them that their journey does not stop when their sport ends. Sharing my knowledge on what I've learned along my journey beyond sports can inform those who are unaware of the resources and opportunities available to them. Out of this journey, Ninety8Percent was birthed.

> " I didn't think it was possible for someone like me, with a sociology degree and a horrible graduating GPA, to make it into a profession like consulting and excel in the workplace with a competitive salary. "

Ninety8Percent's goal is to empower athletes to share their stories and to inspire others who may be on a similar journey, or who are just trying to figure life out. The platform provides a place for athletes to find resources such as career opportunities, links to courses, athletes' stories, and so much more that they may have never been exposed to in college.

May Ninety8Percent be a reminder to anyone reading my story that your story is unique, meaningful, and inspiring, and it can impact the lives of many others.

ABOUT DEPHANIE

As a collegiate student-athlete at UCLA, Dephanie Adeyemi struggled with finding her path and transitioning into a world without a team, coaches, and trainers to support her journey. Although track and field had been a monumental part of her life, she learned that she needed to shift her priorities and mindset and accept that being an athlete wasn't her full identity.

Frustrated with the lack of resources and network after no longer wanting to pursue medicine after graduation, Dephanie found her way into multiple industries within the corporate space including marketing, advertising, and management consulting.

Through her years of work experience, she learned two things. The first was how to navigate the corporate world with limited experience. The second was that people are interested in an NCAA athlete's story.

Dephanie founded the platform Ninety8Percent to empower athletes in different stages of life and to encourage them to share their story. She believes that every story is unique, meaningful, and inspiring and has the potential to change the life of someone else who may be going through a similar journey.

She currently spends her time connecting with and interviewing athletes and sharing resources that help athletes attain a smoother transition from college sports to life without sports. Ninety8Percent can be found on all platforms.

Chapter 6

LIVE YOUR LIFE GUIDED BY INTUITION
BY DAVID KARASEK

As athletes, we often go through life without truly appreciating some of the simple assumptions we subscribed to in order to get results. For example, we know that our true, natural instincts only emerge in their full power when our minds are still. If you want a real peak performance experience, your mind has to be present, and it has to be quiet.

We also commonly fail to recognize that these assumptions apply to our lives after professional sports, as well. Let me give you an example. Imagine you are living in New York and you want to drive to Boston, but you don't know the roads well. What do you do?

Usually, you would enter the destination in your phone's navigation app and follow the directions. Your phone determines the route by simply pinpointing your current location in New York and then showing you the fastest way to Boston. Right?

For a GPS system to work, it needs a minimum of two points: the destination and the current location. If it knows that you're in New York but you don't have a destination, it's not going to give you any instructions, and you will not arrive anywhere.

On the other hand, if it knows that you want to go to Boston, but doesn't know your current location, it won't know where to start routing your trip.

Do you see the similarity between this scenario and the process of human goal-setting? In order to reach a desired destination (or goal), we need both a plan for where we want to go *and* an understanding of the current reality, or our starting point. The more accurate these two points are, the faster we'll arrive at the destination, and the smoother our journey will be.

Most people will agree that a GPS is useless unless it's given a final destination. Yet, if you ask random people on the street what their vision is, you rarely get a congruent and authentic answer. The same goes for their current reality and where they stand compared to their vision if they even have one. Do you notice the obvious disconnect between what we intellectually understand and what we actually implement in our lives?

I would like to touch upon another powerful principle that athletes should know inside and out from our competitive years. Unfortunately, it is also one we often fail to apply in the business world. I first discovered this phenomenon in myself when I, for the first time in my life, failed to recreate the success I was used to from swimming. My theory is now being confirmed by many of my private clients who find themselves in a similar transition into a new chapter of life. It is the benefit of being guided by intuition.

To start, let's explore why it is easier to be guided by intuition as an athlete than as a businessman or woman. Toward the end of the chapter, I will introduce you to a simple bridge that you can utilize to connect with your intuition once again, just as you did during your career in sports.

It will allow you to apply your unique, athletically minded insight into everything that you choose to do. As so often, it's not about learning something new. Rather, it's rediscovering and mastering what you already know.

While actively competing, I often didn't appreciate how privileged I was to receive quick and direct feedback on what was working and what wasn't. The results never lied. In sports, it is easy to quantify your results and the progress you're making. That's an important advantage compared to the world beyond sports; it allowed me to try new things, do more of what was working, and change the things that were not working.

The constant feedback helped me understand how I was doing and what I was learning. It gave me an accurate idea of my current position, and I could immediately correct course if I got off track. Of course, like all athletes, I went off track many times during my sports career.

However, knowing exactly where I was in terms of skill and effort meant I recognized myself as the primary source of my outcomes. I happily took more self-responsibility, and, therefore, felt more in control of my path and success.

As an athlete, I'm sure you relate to this. When you're transitioning into the business world, everything changes. The feedback isn't so direct anymore, includes a lot of outside variables, and comes with a time lag. Suddenly, you are dealing with variables like your boss, colleagues, the CEO, your clients, and the overall economy. It becomes difficult to identify your exact position, both personally and professionally.

When I transitioned out of swimming and into the world of finance, I quickly noticed that I wasn't as successful in my new environment— at least not in the timeframe I had expected. I slipped into a victim role, assigning the power outside of myself as I began to point fingers at my circumstances. My boss didn't value my contributions, my colleagues were selfish, our clients were risk-averse, the economy sucked ... I could go on with all the excuses I had at the time.

I didn't fall into a depression, but I did begin to feel powerless. I started to lose faith in my own ability to create the career of my dreams. There were too many variables outside of my control, and I had a hard time dealing with this new reality. I distracted myself by staying out late with friends, often drinking until the early hours of the morning.

Can you see how I was desperately looking for orientation in my situation? I was trying to regain the level of control that I was used to and resorting to bad, unhealthy, or downright damaging habits to do so. When I didn't get the outcome I wanted, I immediately assigned the blame to someone other than myself. This search for control turned out to be useless. The reality is we can't control everything, even if we want to.

" When you're transitioning into the business world, everything changes. "

I was wasting so much of my energy on trying to successfully navigate my circumstances that I lost sight of the inspired life I truly wanted to live. It was exactly at that time when a sixty-five-year-old man approached me here in Zurich where I live and invited me to a cup of tea. He was an Englishman with a thick British accent, but I could tell he was very knowledgeable, so I happily agreed. I found it intriguing because I'd never been invited for tea in my life—usually, it would be coffee or beer.

So, we sat down in a nice hotel by lake Zurich, and he asked me to look around and notice that everything that wasn't green or grown by Mother Nature we, human beings, created with our own minds. I absorbed his words in silence and tried to wrap my head around what he had just said.

He continued, "We can not only create things but also have the capability to create the life that we want."

What he said was a huge stretch for my level of thinking, but it intrigued me so much that I couldn't sleep that night. I felt like a little kid who had just seen the most amazing magic show but had no access to YouTube to find out how the tricks were done.

The following morning, I signed up for one-on-one coaching with the Englishman, and in my first lesson, he taught me how to let go and give up my need for control. It's very important to note that his advice wasn't to focus on what *was* in my control but to give up control *altogether*. So, that meant I had to learn to give up control over situations that actually felt like they *were* in my control. I know that sounds crazy, but let's dig deeper.

You see, if you are driven by the need to control things, you are cutting yourself off from any solutions other than what you can work out in your mind. Many times, you will find that these alternative solutions might be better than what you come up with on your own. By trying to work everything out ourselves, we often overthink things. As you probably already know from your time in sports, overthinking is the enemy of peak performance. This principle remains the same when it comes to business.

Consider the time you spent as an infant.

When you began to walk as a one-year-old child, do you remember how you learned? Did you use a set of instructions from your mom or dad and then try to execute it? Of course not! You couldn't even speak a language at that time. Our natural instinctive abilities, which we learn before the age of consciousness, are not taught to us through language. So, how do babies learn to walk? In fact, how do babies learn to do anything without any instructions?

It's quite a miracle when you think about it. The baby first gets a very clear idea of what they want to learn. They look at their parents and gain a clear mental image of the desired outcome: walking upright on two legs. After many failures and not a single complaint, the baby eventually takes its first steps.

Appreciate that the baby doesn't respond to instructions such as, "Move your right foot three inches forward, and don't forget to put the bodyweight on the left side, child!"

I know this sounds ridiculous, but the absence of instructions is significant when you consider how important they are to fully grown, thinking adults.

You know what's also absent? Judgment!

The baby doesn't judge itself. They may fall down or stumble a hundred times before successfully taking a single step, but they never feel embarrassed about it. Have you ever heard of a parent giving a one-year-old a hard time for being unsteady on their feet? So, in addition to no instructions, there is also no judgment in this scenario. We can observe that in the absence of these two things, we create the most natural and efficient learning environment.

The parents and anyone else witnessing the baby's progress trust in their natural ability to follow their instincts to learn how to walk. In the absence of thought, there is no room for judgment, and there is no urge or need to be in control.

Dr. Joe Dispenza, one of the leading experts in the field of meditation and its benefits, states that the thinking mind operates at 2,000 bits of data per second, whereas the sub-conscious mind works at 400 billion bits of data per second. That should be indication enough of the absolutely magnificent and marvelous supercomputer we all possess inside of us. It is also one that rapidly learns and creates when given the trust and space to do so.

I want you to imagine a ten-year-old child (Joe) who is taking tennis lessons to improve his serve. The coach can take two very different approaches here.

The first approach is what we see frequently today. The coach will give a set of instructions that engage Joe's mind.

"Hold the wrist firm, and don't move the weight forward too early" are common instructions to get our controlling mind going. Joe is bombarded with a series of how-to instructions which, with repeated failures to successfully serve, only leave him with the feeling that he will never get it right. All of this leads to overthinking.

The second approach is different because it looks to engage Joe's natural learning capabilities and not the thinking mind. The easiest way for the coach to do that is to simply show a few serves and ask Joe to observe without any verbal instructions.

Joe can then create a mental image of the serve before attempting to hit a few of them. He will objectively look at the outcome of his serves, and his body will make the necessary adjustments in order to replicate the correct version. The key here is non-judgmental observation. In this approach, Joe is given the opportunity for trial and error without judgment.

There's a good story about Roger Federer, who is considered one of the all-time greats in tennis. I'm a huge fan because he's Swiss, and I got to meet him at the 2012 Olympic Games in London. For thirty years before Roger's time, everyone in tennis was teaching the two-handed backhand. They thought that was the best way to hit a backhand.

But, Roger's coach was special. He asked Roger to hit the backhand in the way that felt most natural to him. Since he was free from how-to instructions and given the space to experiment instinctively, he invented the one-handed backhand. To this day, it is his secret weapon and probably the best backhand in tennis. It's absolutely amazing what we can come up with if we let go of control and trust our natural abilities instead.

We've all been in that state of peak performance where we felt "in the zone," totally focused, yet relaxed at the same time. These moments come when the mind is quiet. The thinking mind has suspended the need to control and has successfully put trust in our natural ability to achieve a successful outcome. In this state, instead of working with only 2,000 data bits to solve a problem, we're activating more of the 400 billion data bits that are available to us every second.

Below are a few simple steps that will help you engage your marvelous natural abilities:

Step 1: Stop self-judgment. Here in the first step, the most important thing is to create an accelerated learning environment where you are allowed to make mistakes and fail. When you are allowed to fail, you will be relaxed and curious. And when you are curious, you will learn faster, which is what we want. Most of us athletes are our own hardest critics. Would you agree?

What helped me understand that judging myself is actually self-destructive to a certain degree was when I learned that all my judgments have their origin in what happened to me in the *past*.

These judgments are not a good indication of what's really going on or of what I can achieve in the future. I knew I wanted my future to be different from my past, so the simple and obvious solution was to just let go of judgments.

Step 2: Create a clear mental image of the desired outcome.

Step 3: Experiment and let it happen. With a powerful mental image planted in your consciousness, it's now time to experiment and build confidence in your natural abilities. You want to operate with a firm belief in yourself and faith in your abilities to create what you love. There is a quote from Bob Proctor, who was featured in the hit movie *The Secret,* that I'd like you to memorize if you can:

"Fear and faith both demand you believe in something you cannot see. You choose!"

Choose faith here.

Step 4: Observe non-judgmentally and improve. If it's this simple, why do adults struggle so much to execute this natural process we all followed as children? Why do we have such a hard time letting go of control, even though we understand how powerful our natural abilities are?

The reason is simple: Being in control pleases your ego. It feels like it's important because it's in control. However, that sense of control is dangerous and keeps you operating with 2,000 bits of information when you could be using much more.

I invite you to take a moment and answer this series of questions as honestly as you can:

- Would you rather be right or happy?
- Who is your harshest critic?
- What is your harshest critic telling you?
- Where is this information coming from?
- Would you bet money that this information is true and accurately describes what you do?
- I'm asking again, would you rather be right or happy?
- Do you believe that your intuition has power and knows what's best for you?
- After reading this chapter, what's the first step that you can take to build trust in your natural abilities?

Let me close this chapter by illustrating a second framework from our daily lives, similar to the GPS analogy, that will serve as the bridge connecting us to our natural abilities and intuition once again.

I currently live in Switzerland, and the summer of 2021 has so far been the worst in terms of weather. It has rained more and been colder than any year since 1908. That qualifies as once-in-a-lifetime shitty weather, doesn't it? Despite that, is it safe for me to assume that the sun is behind the clouds, even if I can't see it right now?

Absolutely!

It makes total sense to assume that. We don't think twice about the fact that the sun rises and sets every day, even when it is out of sight. If we didn't subscribe to that concept, we would wake each rainy, gray day and panic, wondering when we might see the sun again. Through this assumption, we are automatically more relaxed and don't need to see the sun every day to know that it's still there. The power is in the assumption.

Similarly, you can assume that your intuition is all-knowing and wants the best for you. Through that trust, you can let go of the need to control and put the power in your natural abilities instead. Just as you know the sun is behind the clouds, also know that your natural instincts are behind your thinking mind.

When you allow your thinking mind to let go of control, your intuition will emerge and guide you in every challenge you undertake. So, this is the bridge that I use for myself, and all my clients, to quickly connect with our natural abilities:

Assume that you have powerful natural abilities. Assume, and then roll with it. Give up the need to control, know your desired outcome, and let it happen. It is really that simple! The power is in the assumption. It's now okay to give up control because we know we prepared the fertile grounds for our all-powerful natural abilities to emerge.

Through this method, we can tune into our athletic mindset once again fully in charge of our own lives and outcomes, deeply trusting in our own intuitions, and objectively observant of our actions in a way that stimulates growth and learning.

In the work that I do, we have a beautiful definition of magic. It is "the ability to live a life guided by intuition." When we live in this way, we are self-referenced. We get our inspiration from inside ourselves. All the power that was previously assigned outside of us now comes back to us, and that is a beautiful and very empowering thing.

We all had the ability to live a life guided by intuition when we were kids. Finding that way of life again is not so much about learning something new than it is about becoming aware of a few habits (the need to control, overthinking, etc.) that we picked up along the way.

It's about realizing that many of them don't serve us in our current situation and that we have the power to unlearn them. And, when we build trust in our natural abilities, even the rainiest and coldest summer days can't diminish our faith that everything, somehow, ends up in our best interest—as long as we know what we really want.

ABOUT DAVID

David Karasek is a former Olympic swimmer for Switzerland. When his swimming career ended, David could not recreate the success he'd had as a swimmer in the business world. Because he was so used to getting immediate and direct feedback from sports, he never fully developed a mechanism to cope with the more complex and indirect nature of the workforce.

After several years of feeling powerless, David began to give up his need for control and, thereby, created the space for his intuition to emerge. He now helps professional athletes and their coaches stop overthinking and prepare the grounds for intense peak performance experiences.

It's become his personal mission and passion to reach out and help others perform better under pressure so they can give more to themselves, their teams, families, and everyone who supports them. David is also the founder of The Tribe of Athletes, a sports community dedicated to mastering the journey to inner greatness.

Chapter 7

BUILT ON A CRACKED FOUNDATION

BY ELLEN RENK

You can never quite pinpoint how those relationships begin—the ones that seem to come about so slowly but all at once at the same time. You're aware of their beginnings, but, by the time you're truly in it, you have no idea what happened. Many times, these relationships are amazing. They're the stuff romance novels, fairy tales, and rom-coms are made of. You know, the ones you can't stop watching no matter how bad the acting is (looking at you, Lifetime movies).

I've been through my fair share of these relationships. I fell into high school "love," did the long-distance college thing, and dated the narcissistic guy whom I thought was the greatest. None of those pairings would win me an award for "best relationship of the year," but I am fortunate to look back and say that all of them were pretty harmless in the grand scheme of things.

Then, there were the relationships that aren't so harmless—the ones that aren't often written about, romanticized, or shown on the movie screens. They aren't something you learn about growing up. You aren't told how common they are, how to spot the warning signs, or how to stop them before you get too deep. And, unfortunately, if you're like me, you inadvertently stumble into them.

That's where this story begins.

Of all the relationships I have built in my life, none of them were quite as impactful (or toxic) as the one in which I found myself during my sophomore year of college. Its true beginnings had started back in high school, but, as I said, these kinds of affairs tend to happen both slowly and all at once. Despite what you are probably thinking, I'm not talking about a romantic relationship with a boy.

I'm talking about my relationship with my body and what became an extremely toxic relationship with food, orthorexia, and bulimia. All of it started with the simple desire to enhance my athletic performance.

I don't want to tell you a heroic story about how I beat this relationship. Everyone wants to hear about the success, the glory, but I think there's more to be gained from understanding *how* a person's story began and where it took a turn for the worse—specifically, all of the unassuming red flags that grew exponentially to become one of the biggest things they would ever face. Enough hero stories. Give me a good origin story. That's where the meat is! Any other Marvel or DC fans out there?

I want you to truly understand the roots of my experience and how the small fissures in the foundation of my self-worth and body image would become the crippling issues I faced as an athlete and after graduation. So, I'm going to walk you through the events that led to what became, from a mental health and soul perspective, the most pivotal six years of my life.

Like the rest of the authors who contributed to this work, I have been an athlete my whole life. My mom likes to joke that I came out running, feet first. From as far back as I can remember, I was running around. I would run to a friend's house down the street, I ran as a pinch-runner in softball, and I was always quick on my feet to retrieve fly balls at my older brother, Sam's, baseball games.

My proudest memory was racing my brother in a 100-meter dash in the street in front of my house. I was gaining on him at the end, and I almost beat him ... barefoot.

Running meant more to me than feeling proud; I remember an immense amount of joy, as well. Standing there in the street, hands on my knees, the soles of my feet hot from the concrete, I sported an *I can't believe it was so close* smile on my face.

Just pure joy; that's what I felt while playing sports when I was younger. Yes, I always wanted to win, but I also just *loved* playing. It was fun to play. You get a feeling playing sports that you can't find anywhere else. Those moments when you're lost to the rest of the world and completely absorbed in the task at hand; that feeling of cohesion between mind, body, and sport is what Cory Camp refers to as *flow*.

When I was little, finding that flow was my jam. However, as I got older, I lost that sense of joy in the sports I played. It wasn't that I didn't think it was fun anymore. I simply had the realization that it's also fun to win. With that, joy took a backseat to performance, and, instead of playing for the joy of it, I started playing to win.

Fast forward to my senior year of high school, basketball season. I hadn't played basketball the year before because I was focusing on track. Junior year is pivotal for scholarship offers, and I had signed with Northern Illinois University on a full-ride scholarship to do long and triple jump. For senior year, I decided to play basketball again just for fun and as one last hurrah for that young kid in me who still wanted to find joy in sports.

That was the year I truly began noticing my body. For all the women reading this, you probably remember a similar timeframe. Hormones start kicking in, your metabolism is no longer raging, and you can no longer smash a whole box of cereal as a snack without thinking about it. The negative thoughts started small.

I wore a pair of tight spandex compressions underneath my basketball shorts, and I began to notice a little bit of my stomach roll over the waistband when I sat down during practice.

That was all it was, the tiniest of catalysts, but it was enough to spur a hyper-awareness about my body. I began looking at other girls and their bodies, comparing myself. As a young woman who identified as an athlete and grew up playing sports with my brother and his friends, I didn't have a lot of female influences.

I was already self-conscious about not feeling *feminine* enough. Now, with my body changing in very feminine ways that felt foreign to me, I began to wonder why this small roll made me feel so gross. I looked at other girls in my class who were bigger than me, and I thought they were beautiful, but I didn't feel beautiful.

How could my perception of myself be so different from my perception of others?

I didn't know then that this was something so many of us struggle with: hypercriticism of our own bodies and body dysmorphia. Nor did I know that these small nitpicks would begin to seep into every aspect of my mind, poisoning my self-esteem and sapping the joy from my daily life.

That same year, I found out I was favored to win State in both long jump and triple jump. I was ecstatic, and I wanted to do everything in my power to win. I had ranked second for two years, and I was ready to finally nab that top podium spot. With basketball season coming to an end and track on the horizon, I devised the following plan to push myself and reach peak physical condition:

5. Wake up every morning at six and either run or do P90x (a rigorous workout regimen) in the basement before school. My alarm said, "Wake up! Win State!"

6. Print out the nutrition plan from P90x, buy every ingredient on the grocery list and give up any food that wasn't included. I had one last waffle bowl from Dairy Queen before saying goodbye to all sweets.

7. Continue to drive an hour every other weekend to get one-on-one lessons from a coach from Illinois Wesleyan (I had been doing this during the season since sophomore year).

8. Never miss a workout, skip practice, or deviate from my meal plan. Be dedicated. No regrets.

I didn't know it then, but this plan initiated a massive shift in my relationship with food and exemplified some of my obsessive tendencies. I no longer was enjoying food—it was fuel. I saw sweets as the enemy as if one chocolate chip cookie would be the reason I didn't win state. Even one bite was off-limits.

This level of dedication also led to me tying my self-worth and value into performance. When you put your whole heart into something, you give it a lot of power. It's the reason breakups can be so devastating. You give everything to someone, and, if it doesn't work out, you begin to question,

Was it me? Was it something I did? What does this mean about me? What could I have done differently? Who am I without them?

The same line of thinking occurs for athletes. When you pour your heart into a sport in an effort to increase your performance, and then you don't perform the way you wanted to, you begin to question yourself on a soul-deep level.

That's what happened to me after sectionals that year. I had already qualified in both long and triple jump for state with marks that would bring me in ranked first. The last event I had was a 4 x 100-meter relay, which I was running to support some younger girls on the team getting experience in the race. Ten feet before the finish line, I felt a pop in my hamstring, and my whole world shifted to slow motion. I remember limping over the finish line, looking across the track, and seeing my dad. His face was still and scared. I will always remember the worry in his eyes as he watched me hobble off the track.

For the first few moments, I was in utter shock and emotionless. I slumped down on the concrete, holding my leg, and began crying. "I don't understand. What does this mean?" I asked through sobs to my teammates around me. It wasn't long until my parents, coaches, and the athletic trainer were there. The good news was that I hadn't torn anything, and it was likely a bad pull. The bad news was that I had absolutely no idea what it meant for me.

I spent the next two weeks going to physical therapy twice a day to try and rehab my hamstring to compete at state. Looking back, I don't think anyone thought it was possible to recover in such a short amount of time, but they supported me in trying to still make my dream a reality. It didn't work. Instead of competing, I sat by the pit and supported the other girls as they tried to earn their spot on the podium.

I remember standing out on the track at Eastern Illinois, trying to do a run-through to see if I could complete just one jump. I didn't make it eight steps before having to pull up. When we all gathered together with the official to begin, he turned to me and asked me to remove my earrings because I wouldn't be able to compete with them in. I began crying. It didn't matter. I would only be watching.

I was absolutely devastated. The dream I had worked years for felt like it was ripped out from underneath me in one moment. It felt unfair and cruel, and I was so lost. But, as devastated as I was, I didn't face it head-on. If you're an athlete, chances are you know all too well about the lack of mental health awareness and support for athletes in this kind of situation, and it was no different for me back then. I did what most athletes do in situations like this; I buried my emotions.

I didn't confront my feelings of failure and the sadness I felt about having tried so hard and fallen short. I didn't realize that I was struggling with questioning who I was and my worth if I wasn't standing on the podium. I didn't lean into the fact that I was more than an athlete, and this small event in my life didn't speak to who I was or what I was capable of. Instead, I told myself that high school state was nothing compared to DI track and field, and I had a world of opportunity in front of me to achieve even bigger things in the next four years. I thought I could still be the best, so I turned my sights toward college.

Full-ride Division I athletics is no joke. They say one percent of athletes compete in D1, and an even smaller percentage receive full rides. No pressure, right? Looking back, I remember telling everyone how excited I was. I felt so proud when the local newspaper featured the story of my commitment, and I was in awe as I walked around the athletic facilities at the college.

Not to mention the perks! The athletes were provided loads of Adidas clothing every year for track, I lived in a brand-new dorm with my own room and bathroom, and we were given free chocolate milk in the weight room (this, above all, was my favorite). It was easy to get caught up in the excitement and shiny exterior of D1 track and field, which made it even easier to mask how I was truly feeling.

Inside, I was terrified of not stacking up, performing below average, and not being good enough. I didn't know how well I would perform after my hamstring injury and was terrified of letting myself and everyone else down.

I wish this was the part of the story where I tell you how I was wrong and that I should have believed in myself, but it's not. Nothing about my freshman year went how I dreamed it would, and I ended up spiraling into a depression during my first semester. This left me utterly confused and alone.

I mentioned before that the mental health of athletes isn't something that's widely talked about. It's on the rise now with people like Victoria Garrick taking a stand and moments like that of Simone Biles in Tokyo finding the spotlight. But, back in 2016, at a time when I needed it most, mental health support didn't exist for athletes. Or, at least, it wasn't present enough for me to know how to find it.

The pressure to perform was high, and I just wasn't living up to my performance pre-hamstring injury. I was also having a difficult time transitioning to college life, which weighed on me and affected my performance. My coaches made it very clear that I had to do better. That winter, we took a trip to Florida to compete at a track meet, a sort of warm-up for the outdoor season to come.

I didn't feel well at the track meet. My throat was dry; I felt fatigued and slow. I remember constantly grabbing tiny cups of water to soothe my throat, but even swallowing was painful. My performance that day was terrible, and I remember my coaches sitting me down afterward, telling me that it was unacceptable and that I needed to jump better. They didn't seem to care that I wasn't feeling well and had a no excuses attitude.

We flew back to Illinois and hopped on the bus back to NIU, and I remember texting my mom, telling her everything. I was so upset emotionally and physically felt like death. She picked me up as soon as we got back, drove me the forty-five minutes to my hometown, and took me to the emergency room. I had pneumonia.

Let that sink in. I had pneumonia and still competed in my track meet, but, to my coaches, there were no excuses. Sure, they didn't *know* how bad it was, but that's because they weren't listening. It felt like they only cared about my performance, not my physical health, my mental health, or how I was feeling. That experience made me feel small, less than, and like my value to them and my team truly only came through performing well. I felt like a failure, and I had nobody to talk to about it.

This was the first time I had been away from home without my parents, whom I have always been close to. I had yet to make any friends on the track team. Most of my friends were male wrestlers, and I didn't feel I could open up to them. I remember spending nights crying myself to sleep, confused about how I was feeling.

Shouldn't I be happy? This is supposed to be everything I ever wanted. I am the one percent. What's wrong with me?

It was around this time that my coach called me into her office for a short conversation. It lasted only a few moments that she probably didn't think twice about, but they changed my life.

"You've gained five pounds since coming here," she told me.

I had weighed in when I arrived on campus at a whopping 135 but hadn't thought much about my weight since then. She had evidently been monitoring it and told me that I needed to lose weight to jump better. It's important to note that this woman was an Olympian high jumper, and I had incredible respect for her opinions. After all, she had done what I could only dream of.

She told me, with her golden opinion, that I should push a little less in the weight room. I had been putting in some extra work at the time to try to increase my strength in order to jump better. I should stop that.

She also told me, "Stop eating things like pasta in the cafeteria. That's for girls on the cross-country team." Then, she sent me on my way.

That marked the first time someone told me my body needed to change in order to perform better, that I should lose weight in order to become whom I needed to succeed.

In high school, I tiptoed around the idea that nutrition could influence my body shape and performance. It was the beginning of an altered relationship with food and my body, but by no means was it truly disordered. It was in that moment at NIU, with my coach looking at me disapprovingly from across her office, when the dynamic changed.

I internalized her words as telling me that, in order to live up to her standards, to compete in D1, to jump better, to reach my goals, and be worthy of being on the team, I needed to change my body.

So, I decided that was what I would do. This was the answer to my unhappiness. If I could lose those five pounds, then I'd jump better, which would make me feel better, which would make me happy again. The next six years of my life would revolve around this theme: lose weight, perform better, feel better about myself, be happier.

Or, just slightly simplified: lose weight, be happier.

I could write a whole book about the fallout that was the rest of my freshman year. What you need to know for the sake of this story is that I continued to spiral further into depression. I felt lost and alone. I wasn't living up to the standard my coaches set for me, which curated a feeling of failure that seeped into the depths of my self-worth. I was living as a shell of myself, not truly present in anything I did.

My mom noticed the shift during Christmas break. I wasn't speaking much, spent a lot of time alone, and was barely eating. She was incredibly worried about me and began asking questions. I opened up about how I was feeling, and one night out of the blue, I brought up the idea of transferring.

It's not clear when I started considering leaving, but the mere thought of putting NIU in my past felt like a breath of fresh air to me. I blamed my environment for how I was feeling, unaware that the real issue was my internal beliefs around my identity and self-worth. I thought if I moved schools I would feel better.

Mom supported this idea, but my dad did not. It was the only time in my life that I remember my parents fighting. My dad didn't understand my desire to transfer and thought I should stay and work through what I was feeling. My mom wanted nothing else but to make my pain go away, and supported my desire to change schools; she, too, believed it would be the change I needed.

The air in our house was constantly heavy as we moved through making this decision. It was hands down the most tumultuous, emotional, and stressful time of my life so far. It divided my family and put a strain on us that I will forever regret.

In the end, I transferred to Illinois Wesleyan University. I previously mentioned I had taken one-on-one lessons from a coach during high school, and that coach was the head of the women's track and field team at IWU. This made the transfer very easy and comfortable for me, as I felt like I already belonged there after spending many weekends on campus during high school. But amidst this sense of belonging, a part of me was empty.

Even though it's what I chose, I hated that I gave up a full-ride scholarship. I felt I failed myself and everyone who supported me, even if they would never admit it. This deep sense of failure led me to put more pressure on myself to succeed as an athlete at IWU. As a D3 school, I had the chance to be a national champion. If I could do that, I would prove that the transfer was worth it.

Now a sophomore at IWU, with this increased sense of urgency to perform, I went back to the conversation with my coach at NIU and focused on losing weight. I pinched, poked, and prodded the areas of fat I thought needed to be gone. My meals were small, my workouts were long, and I never drank or went out to social events. Every time I walked past a mirror, I checked my reflection, often staring for long periods of time, assessing my body, and analyzing what I felt should change. My body was my enemy and if I could change it, everything would get better.

Turns out this was harder to do than I thought. Despite my efforts to lose weight, my performance was suffering, and with it so was my mental health. Looking back, my dad was right in that transferring was me running from what I was feeling internally.

I changed schools to get out from under the weight of the depression and anxiety I felt every day, but all the emotions and mental health issues I was facing at NIU followed me downstate to Wesleyan. In fact, they were made worse as I continued to put more pressure on myself to become a national champion.

It was during my junior year that my eating disorder truly took over my life. I obsessed over every piece of food that I ate. All I thought about was my next meal or workout. I would restrict myself, eating cucumbers and deli turkey for breakfast, and always walking with an Ultra Zero Monster in my hand to suppress my appetite. Calorie counting, Vitamix shakes, Paleo, Zone Diet, carb cycling; I tried them all.

Despite my efforts, I was struggling to even qualify for nationals, and I felt I was letting myself and everyone else down. Who was I and what was I worth if I couldn't qualify? An empty feeling filled my gut everywhere I went. I absolutely hated this feeling, and so I fell deeper and deeper into what I believed would help me find a sense of worth again: controlling food and my body.

I thought, *if only I could lose the weight and go to Nationals, it would make me feel like I was worth something.*

I internalized this thought until I believed it to be true. I had no self-worth outside of how I looked and performed. This "truth" was the unwavering spark that fueled my eating disorder that lasted another five years.

During that time in my junior year, I wanted to talk to someone about what I was going through but didn't know how. Outside of my coach's "door always open" policy, I wasn't sure where to turn. (And, let's be honest. What female is going to take up the offer to tell a male coach about their body image issues?)

While I used controlling food as a coping mechanism, I also had other means of running away from and numbing my feelings. I have never shared some of these with anyone until now, but here are a few of the behaviors I used in the coming years to hide my deep feelings of failure, sadness, inadequacy, and low self-worth:

- Distancing myself from friendships, avoiding social events, and not allowing myself to develop deeper relationships.
- Taking ill-advised amounts of melatonin at night to avoid lying awake, lonely, depressed, my head always racing.
- Filling my schedule from dusk until dawn with clubs, internships, school, and practice to avoid having space to sit in my feelings.
- Taking prescription anxiety and depression medications, but not utilizing therapy.
- Over-exercising, on average, working out two or three times a day
- Self-harming in small, discreet ways.

You'll notice a lot of these behaviors either kept my brain so occupied that I couldn't face what I was feeling or shut my brain off to do the same.

Often, when we are struggling to feel worthy, confident, and happy, we end up feeling uncomfortable. We feel scared, confused, and lost.

We don't know how to face these struggles, or how to sit with them, so we look for ways to cope. We try to numb and forget the emotions rather than processing and working through them.

A fixation on food and my body became my main coping mechanism. I found comfort in the control, but that's the dangerous thing about coping. It's not always healthy and, often, not a true solution to your problems.

Sometimes, it can even become an addiction. That's how I perceive eating disorders; they are an addiction to some form of self-harm related to food and your body. For me, this materialized in the form of orthorexia and bulimia, and I truly was addicted.

Orthorexia is an obsession with proper or "healthful" eating, and bulimia is an emotional disorder characterized by overeating, followed by periods of purging, vomiting, or fasting. Both are often associated with distorted body image and an extreme desire to lose weight. For me, this meant periods of being very strict about what I was eating, followed by bouts of bingeing and purging.

My eating disorder felt like it began all at once, but the truth is that it took years to fully emerge. Every negative thought that had gone through my mind since the first time I became aware of my stomach during basketball practice played a part in laying the foundation. I didn't wake up one day and decide to start throwing up trays of brownies; the mental breakdown that led me to that point took *years*.

My addiction loomed behind my shoulder every time I felt like I needed to be better and push harder. It was in every moment that led me to value my performance over my health and mental wellbeing. All the years of associating my entire identity with being an athlete and becoming engrossed in the philosophy that the better I performed, the happier I'd be, culminated in an eating disorder that robbed me of my happiness.

This is where you come in, and where you can connect to my story. Even if you never felt the same pressures when it came to your body, or if your relationship with food was never disordered, you're reading this book because you, too, have tied your identity and self-worth into your status as an athlete.

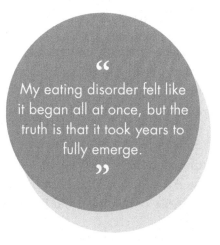

> **"**
> My eating disorder felt like it began all at once, but the truth is that it took years to fully emerge.
> **"**

You can relate to the fact that, for most of your life, your joy and feelings of accomplishment have been centered around playing your sport. Chances are, you have also felt that panicked feeling of "what now?" when faced with the reality that your athletic career is coming to an end.

I reached that point in my life when I was twenty-four. After I graduated, I began competing in CrossFit. Again, my whole identity tied into being an athlete, and this continued to produce an environment focused on success, performance, and my body. Through overtraining and under-eating, I ended up herniating a disc in my back, and I took six months off from serious training. During this time, I engaged in some deep self-reflection, which helped me truly face what I was going through.

I realized a few things. First, was acknowledging that I wasn't having fun anymore. I wasn't happy, and I had lost my love of competition because I was too fixated on the end result. The second realization? I had been bulimic and orthorexic for *six years* and had used my need to perform as an excuse for it. Third, I knew I had to change. The toxic relationship I had with my body, food, and competition had to end. I stepped away from CrossFit and began seeking support for my eating disorder.

Doing so led to my final realization; I had absolutely no idea who I was if I wasn't training or competing. Who was I if I wasn't obsessed with changing my body to perform if I wasn't an athlete?

I told you from the beginning that this wasn't a hero story but an origin story. I don't have near enough space to dive into all the ways I surmounted this loss of identity or the many steps I took to get my life and happiness back. I can tell you that, today, I am over three years binge and purge free. I can also tell you that, even though my eating disorder will forever be a part of me, I have healed my relationship with food and my body.

I now own an online coaching business that helps women build strong bodies and minds. We help them cultivate healthy relationships with food and their bodies while finding confidence not just in how they look, but who they are. I have released all competitive expectations, and I train for the love of it again. And, against all odds, I went with a team to the CrossFit Games this year. Most of all, every day I find joy and purpose in things outside of the gym, which at one point I never thought I would find.

All of this was possible for me because I made the decision that I wanted it. I knew that, in order to find it, I had to stop *coping* with my feelings and face them instead. Until that point, I was building my life on a cracked foundation that I refused to acknowledge.

In order to move forward, I had to work through the moments in my past that I had buried and learn how they had impacted me and what they meant to me. I had to face decisions that I used to hate myself for and forgive. If I truly wanted to live my most joyful, fulfilling life, I had to fully understand what made me *me* before I could change any of it.

That's the message I want you to take from my story. In order to truly grow into who you want to be, you have to face what you're feeling and move through it. You need to realize your present feelings are founded on experiences and emotions from your past that you have allowed to define you, and you have to move through those as well. Often, when we want to redefine ourselves, we look to take action, make a change, and move forward.

The reality is you cannot run from who you were to get to who you want to be. You have to understand the moments that made you who you are today. It gives you perspective and allows you to look at the present with more depth and understanding.

When you can look at your past with understanding, grace, and forgiveness, you allow yourself to move forward in a truly powerful way. That's what I want for you.

So, as you dream of who you want to be, and as you continue to read this book and visualize the person you want to become, I invite you to delve just as deep into the things that made you who you are today. Take the time to think about the moments, memories, and experiences that have shaped you, and ask yourself, what is your origin story?

ABOUT ELLEN

Ellen lives in Minneapolis, Minnesota, and runs on curiosity, snuggles from her golden retriever Tod, and oat milk lattes. She ran D1 track on a full scholarship at Northern Illinois University her freshman year, after which she transferred to Illinois Wesleyan. Ellen was a national qualifier numerous times in long and triple jump and a qualifier in javelin her senior year. The same year, her team won the NCAA DIII Outdoor National Championship.

Post-college, Ellen competed undefeated in both Jiu-Jitsu competitions and kickboxing matches and competed on a team at the 2021 CrossFit Games.

Beyond an athlete, Ellen is a sister, daughter, dog mom, friend, and coach. She loves reading young adult fantasy novels, listening to new music on Spotify, taking photos with her Fuji XT3, plant shopping with friends, and discovering new snacks to try at local co-ops.

After overcoming six years of orthorexia and bulimia, Ellen founded her own coaching company, helping women build strong bodies *and* minds. She is most passionate about helping women find confidence and worth beyond their bodies, and empowering them to be confident in not just how they look, but who they are.

You can find copious photos of Tod and connect with Ellen by reaching out to info@ellenrenk.com or connecting on Instagram (@ ellenrenk) and Facebook (www.facebook.com/ellnrnk).

Chapter 8

WHEREVER YOU WATER IT
BY RACHEL BRETON

"I close my eyes—only for a moment—and the moment's gone."

The familiar and famous line above from the Kansas' song, "Dust in the Wind," replays in my head frequently yet always at different times and moments in my life. The beauty of music is that you can always find lyrics that *get you.*

You can always find that perfect song for what you're feeling in that instant, something that simply says, "Yes, I understand." I believe the same applies to all kinds of athletes, and, for me, this line reflects an important part of the competitive athlete's journey.

As athletes, we live for moments. We push and we grow. We get stronger, we struggle, we suffer, we strive. In 2013, I came across an article by Mark Manson in the Huffington Post entitled, "The Most Important Question You Can Ask Yourself Today."[1] The author asks a loaded question. He doesn't ask what happiness do you want. Instead, he asks, "What pain do you want?"

"What are you willing to struggle for? Because that seems to be a greater determinant of how our lives end up. Everybody wants to have

---

[1] Manson, Mark. "The Most Important Question You Can Ask Your-self Today." *HuffPost*, January 23rd, 2014.

an amazing job and financial independence—but not everyone is willing to suffer through sixty-hour work weeks, long commutes, obnoxious paperwork, to navigate arbitrary corporate hierarchies and the blasé confines of an infinite cubicle hell. People want to be rich without the risk, with the delayed gratification necessary to accumulate wealth."

When I read that, I think back to all the practices, the games into overtime, the staying after, the coming earlier, the "off-seasons" (I know, there really are no off-seasons in soccer), the ups, and the very downs. I think of every fragment of emotion, time, and effort ever put into what we do.

We are okay with the struggle and the pain in that very moment for that fraction of victory, the medal, the teammates, the wave you give to your parents in the crowd, the pre-and post-game locker room hype and banter—the simple happiness of performing for what you love.

As I write about it, I relive the moments. They're raw and real. Although, what happens when all is done? What happens in that very first moment of realization that, one day, it will, in fact, be over?

No one prepares us for *that* pain.

As athletes, we always train and practice like it is going to be *our last*. At first, it's a cute saying to "put life into perspective," maybe hype someone up, or reframe our "purpose," but what happens when it is truly over?

Sometimes, we have an earlier ending than we had envisioned. Sometimes, the road takes an unexpected turn, and your rocketing trajectory comes to a sudden halt due to injury, job opportunities, age, experiences, family, etc. These are unexpected road closures and detours in the journey of the dedicated athlete.

We base our entire life on this sport from a young age. Then, after twenty or more years, it ends. For us soccer players, everything is based on our soccer schedule. When we were younger, we shared a similar daily routine to that of each teammate on our team.

As it progressed, so did our days. If you were serious, you played club, high school, ODP (Olympic Development Program), regional/national team, and so on. It was a tough balancing act with so many tournaments and events, trying hard not to miss too much school as we traveled during the school year to different parts of the nation or even overseas.

There were exams and papers we tried to do in advance, or we made up the work as immediately as practically possible. If we continued this journey, it progressed to college. We chose our classes based on the blocked scheduling our team made and scheduled make-ups for the classes we missed for away games.

Depending on the school you went to, the stakes were even higher. Soccer was life, life was soccer; there was no in-between. We were constantly negotiating the title coined to us as student-athletes and having to face the academic demands that we are athlete-students first.

It never stopped.

After college, some are done playing, while others go further in their soccer careers and capitalize on the opportunity to play overseas, semi-pro, or pro; however, sooner or later, there comes a time when it stops. I have found myself lately repeating the description of a train; you get on, sometimes knowing the stops and destination, while other times you don't know. You try to figure out, are you on the express train, only making a stop here or there, or are you on the local, stopping at every available chance, prolonging the inevitable end of the ride? Whether you are riding express or local, you are heading toward the same destination. The end.

Here lies the true question, which is probably why you picked up this book in the first place: How do you adjust? It is the panic mode everyone goes through, the "Now what?" moment. Yet, despite how common the experience is, many are afraid to provide answers and open up about it.

In response to Mark Manson's question, the competitive athlete accepts and wants the daily pain, the struggles, and the sacrifices that, in the end, become a key part of happiness in the athletic journey. It is what we are happy doing despite the pain.

Novelist and poet, Charles Bukowski says, "If you're going to try, go all the way."

Similarly, Yoda advises, "Do or don't do. There is no try."

Both are the same to me.

With the inevitable, ultimate end in the back of our minds, how could we not go all the way? How could we not see our limitlessness? For those slight moments of happiness, wouldn't we all go through the same pain despite the ending? I would choose this pain every day, in every lifetime, always. It seems so natural to push toward our goals without focusing on all we must overcome to get there. It is not merely about the goals we set for ourselves; it is also about owning the journey itself.

We all wanted the pain because the goal seemed worth it. What many do not foresee, and what no practice, training, or match prepares us for when the "moment's gone," is the letting go of the journey—and yes, even the sweet pain that came with it and that we, in fact, *wanted*.

As athletes move on to other engaging ventures, some do it without the slightest hiccup. For others, it proves to be a bit more challenging than initially anticipated. Many of us find that the experience falls somewhere in between.

I'm writing to you as a retired professional soccer player (Oof, that hurts to write), and it's not easy. I don't care what anyone says, it's not. It doesn't matter how far you went in your sports career. If you loved it, if you chose the pain, it's still a lost love.

Unfortunately, I'm not here to tell you a story about how great life after sport is and how easy of a transition it is. I'm here to tell you the truth, which is there is no recipe or antidote. There's no generic Facebook article with some random odd number on "Seventeen Ways to Let Go of the Identity You Have Resonated with and Built Your Whole Life Around Since You Were Four."

I told you before, it's raw and it's real. Everyone will have similar, yet unique feelings and experiences. That's the beautiful part about it all.

Athletes coming together and normalizing talking about the transition, connecting, and sharing our unique stories and emotions, proves that we all feel the same, that, as alone as we might feel in this "new identity," we are together. As lost as we might be, we are so much very found.

> " With the inevitable, ultimate end in the back of our minds, how could we not go all the way? How could we not see our limitlessness? "

We are never alone.
We are always exactly where we need to be.
We all share the same love and passion.
We all know what it's like to love and lose.

My father would say, "The greatest opponent you'll ever face is yourself." I believe that our faith and vision can move mountains, but, often, the largest mountain in front of us is us. I, too, watch the Euro 2020's, Copa America, and Olympics with almost tears in my eyes, thinking to myself, *Gosh, I love this sport.*

That is something no one can take away from me. It is the understanding that it is something I did, and it will always be a part of me, but it does not define who I am or who I am going to be each and every day.

Closure is relative. It's about growth, and growth isn't in what you gain; it's in what you shed. So, invite the pain with open arms. There will be no salvation without suffering, but in salvation, there is always hope.

Can we make it better? Of course, we can, because the grass is always greener where you water it.

Metamorphosis

At the beginning of tennis champion Andre Agassi's *Open,* he begins his book with a chapter titled, "The End."

Briefly, he describes opening his eyes not knowing where or who he was, curling out of bed, feeling the pain in his body, and being aware of his mind, yet not feeling like his mind—a stranger to himself.

He says, "As this last piece of identity falls into place, I slide to my knees and in a whisper I say: Please let this be over. Then: I'm not ready for it to be over."

I'm constantly asked, "How did you know it was the end of your career?"

Simple. It was when I read those words—another "Dust in the Wind" moment for me. Going back to my train analogy, sometimes you don't know what train you are on ... until you do. I was on the local, soaking in every stop until it was last call, last stop, destination.

In many chats, podcasts, and reflections, I tend to be very honest (a blessing and a curse of mine), and I find myself admitting that I was always one foot in, one foot out. I knew deep down inside I always wanted to be included but not limited to. Though soccer was my everything and definitely my identity (everyone knew me as Soccer Rachel), I knew that soccer was only a tiny fraction of my potential as a human.

Maybe I just have commitment issues (if a therapist is reading this I'm open to some feedback), but truthfully, I feel I was aware of my own mortality way earlier than your average person. It was in the back of my mind in every game, every practice, every day.

But what are you going to do with the other three-quarters of your life? I would whisper to myself.

When did I know? I always knew. Everything we do here is temporary and finite.

"Unlike birds, we confuse our time on Earth, again and again, with obsessions of where we are going—often to the point that we frustrate and stall our human ability to fly. We frequently tame and hush our need to love, to learn, to know the truth of spirit, until we can be assured that our efforts will take us somewhere. All these conditions and hesitations and yes-buts and what-ifs turn the human journey upside down, never letting the heart, wing that it is, truly unfold."

— Mark Nepo, *The Book of Awakening*

We are in bizarre times right now in terms of expectations of where we need to be in life. I think this is where the pressure is heightened (thanks, social media) because we all pretend we have it all together. Let's call a spade a spade; none of us do. Some are better at posting about it, with the best of filters. As Mark Nepo alludes, we are so obsessed and concerned with everything except what is actually happening in real-time.

We have constant distractions, timelines on how things are going to be and should be, and at what time, and we exclaim, "Look at Susie! She bought a house at twenty-five!"

What? Who cares?

I laugh at this as I think of the saying, "We plan and God laughs."

If you are not on this imaginary timeline that, for some reason, we are bouncing off of each other, you are in denial of your adulthood and life.

Just because I was Peter Pan for three Halloweens in a row, a child not wanting to grow up does not mean I'm in denial. I think what stresses us out, especially for a newly to not so newly-retired athlete, is that we feel we're somehow behind.

The what-ifs and now-whats start to haunt us, and we panic. This is where I come in and remind you, again, that your sport is something you did, a verb and a part of your journey, but it is not what will define you.

What *will* define you is you. It's your life. Who do you want to be? How do you want to be remembered? What's your vocation? Start there.

It's all about our vocational identity. The mistake is that we become too attached to our two dimensions, which, ironically, don't exist: our past and our future. I say they don't exist because our past is done. It has no power over the present.

Our future is a hypothetical thought that has yet to come to fruition if it ever will. It's not real. I say this, but I'm guilty at times as I find myself in games or at practices, on a run, or grocery shopping reliving moments over and over again. What does this do for us besides never letting the heart, wing that it is, truly unfold?

Take the past, take the future, and make it now. What can we do right now, with all the tools of life that every sport has taught us? We think we can't be anything without our sport, but that's not true.

Remember when I said soccer is life and life is soccer? That means they are intertwined. That means that it has taught me compassion, love, disdain, hard work, defeat, disappointment, ups and downs, comebacks, and Roman Emperor falls—everything that life is. We are not behind in our experiences.

We were ready before we knew we were, and, ironically, we are the ones who set our limits, not life. So, be like a bird learning to fly, never knowing where it will take you, but trusting in the flight, and how the sky is bountiful and yours.

Now, let's back up; the word retired never comes out of my mouth without distaste. For a very long time, I used to rationalize that I was on a sabbatical. There are days when that little voice says to me, "Maybe one last hoorah. You're still fit and young. This time around, it'll be better. Do it again."

For the moment, I whisper back, "*Girllll,* I just might." It's like that ex you still love and text "hey" with four y's. It's all natural and, again, a way of shedding; it's growth.

My struggle—and I think not just in soccer—was not what I saw, but the story I would tell myself. The way it was supposed to end in my head. They always say it's the story we tell ourselves that haunts us, but I didn't understand that until I did. What time and growth have shown me is that I am the author of my story.

As my parents would say, "Change the narrative."

So, I did. I remembered that I was the girl who'd had perfect attendance in school from kindergarten and all the way through my years in high school. I was the bilingual all As and AP Honors student. I was the girl who played four instruments and learned new ways to dance, who read more than fifty-two books a year and taught herself videography, photography, law, and marketing analytics.

I am the girl who was always "not limited to."

My mom said to me, "As of today, I am the oldest I've ever been, but the youngest I'll ever be."

"But that's every day," I noted the obvious. She looked back, with her sweetest smile that I love so much, and nodded.

Nepo says, "We, like the birds, are meant to fly and sing—that's all—and all our plans and schemes are twigs of nest that, once outgrown, we leave."

All we have, and will ever have, is today. There is no greater agony than burying an untold story inside you. So, outgrow. Fly, sing, and tell it.

ABOUT RACHEL

Professional soccer player and athlete, sports psych mentor, photographer, videographer, and certified strength and conditioning coach Rachel Breton (*b. Kearny, NJ, 4 August 1990*) is best known as the master of all trades. Prior to college, she graduated from high school as an all AP / honors student-athlete, being offered multiple full scholarships to some of the top academic and athletic universities in our nation. Declining early acceptances to some of our nation's Ivy League institutions, she attended both Villanova University and Rutgers University to end with her concentration in English and psychology.

Athletically, she played internationally on the US-Youth National Team pool starting at the age of eleven, competing in countries in the United Kingdom, Brazil, and Russia. In college, she played D1 women's soccer, receiving Big East Academic All-Star Honors through her collegiate seasons. She also had the honor to represent her state, region, and nation professionally in the National Women's Soccer League (Sky Blue FC; NWSL.) and overseas in the Toppserien League in Norway.

During her professional soccer career, Rachel gained unique perspectives, made impactful memories, built unforgettable relationships, and endured authentic struggles for which she is truly grateful. Rachel strives to apply her knowledge and experience in soccer, technology, and psychology to bridge the gap between former athletes and their sense of identity.

In her own words, "Life is about serving others. I love living by my core principles: gratitude, appreciation for God and life, maintaining a healthy and energetic physical body, connecting to our spirits and each other, and perfecting an awareness of the gifts that have been bestowed upon each of us."

Chapter 9

YOU'RE A HUMAN BE-ING BY NIKKI KETT

Yesterday, I woke up to pouring rain. Like the skies, my head was clouded with racing thoughts.

Why aren't you doing more?
You should work out longer today.
You should be over this by now.
What's wrong with you?
How are you possibly going to make this work?

Ah, there it was again. My inner critic woke up and decided to take the wheel. *Not this time. Not anymore.* These thought processes have been driving me for the majority of my life, but instead of believing them and allowing them to drive me into overwhelm, I just let them have their moment without attaching to them. The thing is, I've come to recognize these thoughts. I know what this thinking creates for me, and it's not the way I want to live my life.

I have coached many clients on this exact thing. So often, they get stuck living in a world of pressure, overwhelmed by the thoughts of *"I should."*

Generally, as humans, we become bogged down by the things we think we *should* do in order to feel validated or worthy—the things we hope will finally help us feel like we have done enough to deserve a break. But the thing is, the cycle can be endless.

When it comes to these beliefs, here's a couple of thoughts I want to offer you:

1. You don't have to do anything to be worthy. You just are.
2. You can't create a love you truly enjoy through constant pressure.

Being an athlete has taught you a lot of things: how to work hard, how to win, how to interact with many different people, how to push through challenges and obstacles, and how to manage your time (when there aren't enough hours in the day). However, at the same time you were learning these skills, you may have picked up some beliefs along the way that stopped you from fully enjoying your life and prioritizing your wellbeing.

Here are a few common beliefs that sport may have unintentionally instilled in you:

1. Your worth is based on your performance.
2. Your body should look a certain way.
3. Mental toughness means pushing through everything and anything.
4. If you avoid your emotions, they will go away.
5. There is always more to do. Downtime means you are not working hard enough.

In the midst of my mental tailspin that morning, I had an hour gap in my schedule where I could have forced myself to grind through what was on my plate. But, in my commitment to creating a different result, I chose different actions. I am learning to be with myself when I need to, to sit and process the emotions that come up when I am struggling with something. While it was still drizzling outside, I grabbed my dog and decided to go for a short walk on the beach.

I made a point to leave my phone at home and just *be*. I connected with the water, the boats, and the sand beneath my feet. I sat down, and for five minutes or so, consciously connected with my breath. Just as I felt the pressure beginning to lift from my shoulders, the sun started to peek through the clouds.

I took this as a sign that I was finally on the right track. *And this time, the track doesn't mean following a specific path that gets me to an arbitrary destination.* Instead, the track means slowing down when I feel off. It means taking a moment to come back to the present and connect with what I'm feeling. It means understanding and acknowledging the thoughts that are coming up and, instead of pushing through them, making the intentional choice to tune into my needs before deciding how to proceed.

This track has led me to have compassion for myself and to understand the negative thinking that can relentlessly drive my day-to-day if I don't have awareness. I now choose to allow myself to feel those things and know that no amount of pushing through it or covering it up with work and distractions is going to make it go away.

So, here's my reminder to you: You are a human being, not a human doing.

We live in a culture that is obsessed with productivity and perfection. We create environments where failure and mistakes are viewed as weaknesses.

A coach might tell you to embrace your mistakes but then shame you when you don't perform to a certain level of expectation. You might be told it's okay to fail, but the actions don't reinforce the words. When push comes to shove, we'd rather be perfect so that we don't have to feel the tough emotions that come along with failing. By doing so, we suppress our sadness, anger, grief, and frustration, and an opportunity to redefine failure into growth.

We think that emotions get in the way of our ability to move forward, but this contradicts the great paradox of life: if you want to feel better, you have to open yourself up to feeling and discomfort. When we acknowledge our fears and face them head-on, it gives us the opportunity to move through them into a better version of ourselves.

What's Gotten in the Way of This?

Belonging is a fundamental human need. Evolutionarily, we had to belong to our tribe because it gave us safety and security, and that's why we unconsciously take on the beliefs and mentality of our culture.

Culturally, we get stuck in thinking our worth is in how much we can do. As an athlete, you may have achieved a goal and quickly moved on to the next thing without taking time to celebrate your accomplishment. Upon graduation, there becomes pressure for the next job, the next degree, and we subtly buy into the belief that it's a race to get where we are going.

" You are a human being, not a human doing. "

This way of living will never create a life where you are able to enjoy the process and the journey; it creates an illusion that your worth and happiness are in the outcome.

And it reinforces the idea that you are not good enough until you reach another destination. It may show up as bouncing back and forth between productivity and complete exhaustion and being paralyzed by overwhelming indecision of finding "the right path."

When we don't believe we are enough outside of our achievements, striving for more can become a vicious cycle.

Culturally in the US, we define success for our lives in terms of what we have achieved. Our definition of success under these terms includes status, winning, climbing the professional ladder, and producing. Even if attaining these things means abandoning your emotional wellbeing.

Success does not include moments of weakness and vulnerability under our cultural definitions. We view our emotions and setbacks as weaknesses and a sign that something is wrong with us. We are so afraid of our own emotions that we will do just about anything to avoid them.

Sports teaches that it is important to work incredibly hard to get what you want, but it can also reinforce the idea that we need to push through exhaustion and burnout at personal cost. When we do this to our bodies for years on end, we start to see physical symptoms—injuries, inability to recover from workouts, overtraining syndrome, anxiety, depression, etc.

We have learned that being tough means bypassing what your body is telling you, and to keep going no matter what. But ask yourself this: How are societal expectations of success causing you to sacrifice things your mental wellbeing and other things you enjoy?

For so long, my brain remained focused on results–performance in the pool, my weight, how much money I made, the degrees I had, and how other people saw me. I wasn't acknowledging how burned out I felt from constantly striving. This cycle continued as I transitioned from athlete to coach.

I worked full-time as a college swim coach while simultaneously completing two graduate degrees. Inside of me though I heard the whisper that there had to be more to life than constantly working toward the next achievement.

I wasn't yet aware of the patterns that were driving me, so I continued on. My environmental cues continued to tell me I was on the path to success, but the internal voices were getting so loud that, eventually, I had to listen; no matter how many accomplishments or achievements I accrued, it wasn't going to fulfill me. It wasn't worth abandoning day-to-day happiness.

A New Way of Being

I am still learning how to slow down and enjoy my life, and you can, too. Life is happening every single day, and each moment is more than just a means to an end, an accomplishment, or a statistic. That's not to say those things can't be important, but if you're not truly present and appreciative of the individual moments—enjoying a book in the sun, going for walks in nature, talking to a close friend, traveling somewhere new—you're going to waste a lot of your life being unhappy, burned out, and disconnected from your true desires.

When you allow yourself to slow down and connect to the slower moments of your life, you can hold the duality of emotions –happiness and grief, anxiety and excitement. Life can be embraced as a challenge, but you can also build deep self-trust that you are going to show up for yourself by slowing down and processing when you need it most. You will find that when you open up to all life has to offer, both the good and the bad, your moments of joy will multiply, and your connection to yourself will grow stronger.

I'd like to offer a new definition of success to live by, one that is not contingent on the things we do or the accolades we collect. As a Forever Athlete, I define success as the ability to find joy and fullness of the human experience every day while embracing life's challenges along the way.

By adopting this lifestyle, you can learn to develop a strong relationship with yourself and the confidence that you already have everything you need.

The process of detoxing from some of the harmful messages that athletics and culture have imposed upon you allows you to bring forward your life force where your true self and power lies. It's already within you, so let me introduce some tools to help you bring it out.

Check in with yourself right now without judgment. What are you feeling, and why are you feeling it? If you check in and notice some negative emotion, it doesn't mean that you are weak or that something is wrong with you. It means you have a normal human brain that is trying to protect you.

If you picked up this book, chances are you are a former or current athlete transitioning out of your sport and into the real world. Have you given yourself the chance to truly internalize the impact that transition has made or is making on you?

Our emotions can hold valuable information about how we think and feel about ourselves and the world around us. Understanding our human brain and how it works can allow us more self-compassion instead of constantly running from our emotional world. On average, you have 60,000 thoughts per day.

Of those, about 48,000 are negative. It's no wonder you feel so negative, right? It's normal and doesn't mean anything about *you* as a person. Ultimately, our brain's job is to keep us safe, so it operates according to three motivators:

1. Seek pleasure.
2. Avoid pain.
3. Find the easiest path.

Our brain is programmed to quickly seek out rewards and avoid things that have brought us past pain. Because of this drive, it is constantly calculating risk versus reward. Our reward system in our brain drives behaviors that got rewarded last time and will continue recreating the same pattern over and over again. Your brain gets better at recognizing and recreating patterns of action over time. This is how habits are formed.

So, if it has served you as an athlete to overwork for validation, approval, and to fit in with what everyone else is doing, you will continue this pattern after athletics end. Social belonging is a big motivator for dopamine, and we will do anything to maintain the status quo of achievement even at the cost of self.

We can change this by slowing down enough to listen to what we need and consciously choosing to prioritize our wellbeing. This is uncomfortable to our brain because it fears it won't get a reward, but it is key to rewiring our thinking and habits.

When you find yourself avoiding emotions, you should be asking yourself, "What are you really afraid of feeling?"

The truth is, your negative emotions give insight into your beliefs about yourself.

What if you could pinpoint those thoughts and the meaning behind them, and then ask, "Does this belief serve me?"

Perhaps it would make sense to practice a new belief instead, one that serves you and encourages personal growth. The first step in beginning this constructive thought process is to sit with your emotions and thoroughly process them. You can't work through your limits when you aren't aware of what they are.

Before you can address your beliefs and begin the process of changing them, you must learn how to process the emotions you are feeling. Below are just a few activities you can start with. There are countless ways to process and release your emotions and keep in mind that what works for one person may not work for another. Find what works best for you!

- Breathing exercises
- Journaling or a thought download (to be explained below)
- Working out
- Going for a walk
- Talking to a friend
- Meditation
- Dancing
- Creative expression
- Petting your animals (if you have them)
- Laughter
- Positive social interaction

Shifting Your Beliefs

Culturally, we are taught to connect our worth to our success and our achievement. We look for external validation and approval through our accolades. This is especially true for athletes, who have been conditioned by the praise and admiration of performing well. However, if we can't learn to validate and love ourselves *internally*, all the external validation in the world won't matter, and it will keep us striving from a place of not believing in our worth.

Typically, when I work with clients who are feeling lost and burned out, it's because they have disconnected from themselves and are striving endlessly to perform at the highest level. They mistakenly think that they are going to feel better when they reach some arbitrary destination.

I'm not telling you to stop working hard, but understand that you can work hard *and* prioritize your health and mental wellbeing. You can strive for success *and* emotionally connect with yourself when you know you need a break or a moment to recenter. To allow for this, you have to slow down, step away from the everyday hustle, and identify the limiting beliefs that might be driving you.

The best time to identify these beliefs is when you are stuck in a negative thought loop, especially one that involves a recurring emotion you feel like you can't shake. Take a few minutes right now and write out your thoughts. This is what I call a brain dump or thought download.

- What are you feeling about yourself?
- What are you feeling in general?
- What do you think about your current situation/circumstance?
- What do you think about the people involved?
- What do you think about your feelings? Is there self-judgment?

Don't stop or edit yourself—get it all out onto paper. The simple process of writing this out will help you feel better.

Now you can start to identify the beliefs that are driving these thoughts. Beliefs dictate the way your brain tries to keep you safe or gain you a reward. They don't always serve to create a life that we love or where we honor our own needs.

For example, *I'll be happier when I achieve X, Y, and Z.* This creates a cycle where we are always trying to reach happiness but can't attain it in the moment.

All of our beliefs are *optional.* They are just thoughts we've practiced many times, and, so, they feel real. But you can believe anything you want to believe; the question is whether or not you like the results that these beliefs manifest in your life.

Your belief system drives your thoughts, your thoughts drive your feelings, your feelings influence your actions, and your actions directly determine the results you see in your life.

We get confused when we think that the circumstances of our life determine how we feel about ourselves, but truly it's the way we think. When we don't take a look at the thoughts driving us, we are at the mercy of our human brain and the potentially flawed beliefs we have picked up from our environment.

Remember that you can control your brain; it doesn't have to control you. For example, if the circumstance currently challenging you is your job, let's take a look at how the athletically inclined mind creates a result. One of the common beliefs picked up in sports is, "It's never good enough." How might that belief influence you at work?

Circumstance: Work.

Thoughts: I'll never feel good enough. I need to be better. What will people think of me if I don't perform?

Feelings: Pressured, stressed.

Actions: Becoming overwhelmed, overworking, failure to ask for help, seeking external approval/validation, feeling paralyzed, adopting a perfectionist mentality.

Results: Burnout, feeling lost and disconnected from self.

Our society sends us the message that we need to make it to the next milestone, achievement, degree, etc. before we can truly start to enjoy our lives. We are letting our fear of not being enough drive the bus. But what if you decided it was okay to acknowledge that you are not a robot when it comes to productivity? You can admit to yourself and the people around you that there are more important things in life.

The belief that we are not enough when we are not constantly doing and striving directly results in burnout. This is a common trend I see

118

with my clients who are transitioning from sport or have previously been involved with sports.

The thing is, building a life on the pressure of not being good enough creates a chronic stress response, which results in a negative relationship with self because we disconnect from our true needs in order to belong.

Once you understand how this happens, you can start to shift your thinking. The key is to decide that you are already enough, and always have been, no matter what. By making the conscious choice to accept yourself as you are and tear down the beliefs which have told you otherwise, you can gain a new perspective of the circumstances which previously overwhelmed you. Let's return to the example of your job and observe how adopting a new belief can ultimately lead to new, more desirable results.

Circumstance: Work.

Thoughts: I got this job for a reason, and I am good enough already, but I want to continue growing, or, I am committed to my job, but not at the cost to my wellbeing.

Feelings: Confident, calm, empowered.

Actions: Work hard without second guessing your worth. Make time for things that bring you joy—friends, family, exercise. Trust your journey will unfold as it's meant to. Set boundaries and limits for your work; follow your own path, not what everyone else says you should do.

Results: Create a life that you enjoy while staying connected to yourself and your desires.

Altering your beliefs doesn't mean you'll never experience stress, but the way you treat your relationship with your work and yourself can yield healthier results in your life.

Here's how you can start to reframe some of the potentially harmful beliefs you may carry from your athletic career:

1. ~~Your worth is based on your performance~~. I am already worthy, just by being.
2. ~~Your body should look a certain way~~. My body is so much more than how it looks.
3. ~~Mental toughness means pushing through everything and anything~~. Mental toughness means learning to say when I need to take a break to feel and process my emotions.
4. ~~If I avoid my emotions, they will go away~~. Feeling my emotions helps me move through them.
5. ~~There is always more to do; downtime means I'm not working hard enough~~. There will always be more to do, but having downtime allows me to relax so I can show up and do my best work without burning out.

Think about who you want to be. How does that person show up in the world? What do they feel? How do they think about themselves and their circumstances? It's up to you to validate yourself and direct your thought process in ways that create the positive energy you want in your life.

Take some time to write out five new thoughts that help you connect with the person you want to be. What would that person's thought process be? Put it somewhere you will see it often as a reminder and practice those thoughts every day. Our beliefs are choices, and we can always shift them by first acknowledging and understanding what is driving our feelings.

Building Self-Trust and Confidence

With every small action you take toward building belief in the person you are becoming, you gain a sense of trust and confidence in yourself. You are strengthening new ways of thinking and wiring new connections in your brain. You are creating new ways of *being*.

No person or thing can validate your life for you; you have to do that for yourself. You can do this by consistently taking action with the mindset that you are good enough, no matter what. Even if you don't get it right the first time, or the hundredth time, you're still good enough. Never stop validating who you are, and never stop taking action to become the person you want to be. To build confidence and belief in yourself, you have to do these two things simultaneously.

The most important thing I'd like you to take away from this chapter, in regard to your transition from athlete to Forever Athlete, is that, regardless of your status, achievements, or performance, you offer unique, beautiful value to the world.

Regardless of your flaws, imperfections, past mistakes, and failures, who you already are is amazing. When you build your life from a place of fullness instead of scarcity and lack, you will find true confidence and freedom. Your failures do not define you; they help you grow into the person you want to be.

Life will not be without struggle but know you are strong enough to handle it. You are allowed to feel everything. Continue to build internal trust in yourself, and your path will unfold before your eyes. Changing the inherent beliefs in athletics and society starts with small, individual shifts in action.

It takes one person saying, "I'm not going to work so hard that I ignore my emotional needs and cause myself to burn out. I will prioritize myself and my wellbeing."

When enough people refuse to define success as achievement at the cost of self, eventually, the scales will be tipped. By validating yourself and deciding how you want to think and feel about your life, you are contributing to this change in our culture.

You are a human *being*, not a human doing.

ABOUT NIKKI

Nikki Kett is a former collegiate athlete and was an All-American swimmer at Kenyon College. She worked as a college swimming coach for nine years, working with athletes at Johns Hopkins University, University of Pennsylvania, and, most recently, the University of Michigan. She has seen how the pressure to perform at the highest level impacts student-athletes in the pool and in the classroom, as she has coached multiple D1 NCAA champions and Olympic medalists.

Nikki is passionate about understanding how humans can live at their highest potential and prioritize their wellbeing. She is also invested in determining how leaders can help to create positive, supportive environments for the people around them. Nikki holds two graduate degrees—one in kinesiology (concentrating on sport and health psychology) and one in organizational dynamics. She is also a certified life coach.

She focuses on working with women in their twenties and thirties who desire to relieve stress and burnout and find more confidence and self-trust. In addition, she works with teams and coaches to help athletes nurture their emotional wellbeing and achieve their goals, both at the individual and team levels.

Nikki believes the key to resiliency and stress management is creating environments where emotions are welcomed and addressed in healthy ways, as this is the secret to sustainable growth.

Connect with Nikki:
Instagram: @nikkikettcoaching
Email: nikkikettcoaching@gmail.com

Chapter 10

BEYOND THE COMPETITION

BY SARAH NEAL

When I was four, I began tagging along with my sister to the local ice-skating rink. It was a seasonal facility built in the 1960s with an open end and gaps between the walls, roof, and foundation. Quaint and beloved in the neighborhood, the rink provided lots of happy memories and an outdoorsy, adventurous atmosphere. The building ran a large, recreational skating school that met one day a week and included all levels and ages.

The girls wore uniforms to help create a cohesive community—white turtlenecks, blue polyester skating jumpers, and ribbed sweater tights. You could supplement the group classes by taking private lessons during the crowded public skating sessions. My sister and I loved skating so much that we added several weekly private lessons. I don't know how our parents afforded the lessons on teachers' salaries, but they always sacrificed and did their best to support us.

The ice was terrible (they ran the Zamboni no more than once a day, sometimes less), but the memories from that time are sweet. It was pure, childlike enjoyment, and we had big dreams and lots of freedom. Remembering those early days on the ice reminds me why I fell in love with the sport of figure skating.

It was the eighties and early nineties—the heyday of figure skating with Katarina Witt, Debi Thomas, Kristi Yamaguchi, Michelle Kwan, Nancy and Tonya, Scott Hamilton, and the Battle of the Brians.

In Louisville, the program was relaxed enough that we still got to hang out with our school and neighborhood friends, play outside, try other sports, and visit our grandparents for weeks at a time over the summer. Anyone who was seriously competitive in skating moved away to train.

In the eighth grade, I suffered a freak, non-skating-related accident—I slipped in the wet grass while running down a hill at my friend's house and flipped over a political sign. The accident fractured my pelvis and tore a hamstring.

While I was off the ice, I developed exercise-induced asthma and gained a bit of weight. When I returned, my coach was frustrated that I had to ease my way back into lessons, so she became as passive-aggressive toward me as she had been doting before.

She pitted my best friend and me against each other in an old-school attempt to motivate us, but it backfired. Ultimately, our parents decided that the environment wasn't good for us, and we decided to go elsewhere.

The closest rink that offered the coaching we needed was about ninety minutes away, so I started commuting after school with a couple of younger skaters. Sometimes, another coach from home drove us, and other times, parents carpooled. I felt important—like I was in the big leagues. I lived for skating and learning, and I wanted to go far, whatever that meant.

Although the new rink was more inclusive and competent, I was fighting an uphill battle in training. Not only was I catching up for lost time, but because of the commute, I always arrived late and missed important before-school training hours. I lived on the road—eating, changing clothes, studying, sleeping in the car—and I wasn't able to socialize with friends from either skating *or* school. I felt like an outsider to both worlds.

Not long after making the switch to the new club, I developed severe tendonitis of the ankle. My coach mentioned to my mom that, if I lost a few pounds, it might go away. Influenced by diet culture and the frustration of living with a teenager, my mom told me my coach's advice. That one comment was all I needed to hop on the low-fat craze train of the nineties and start my battle with eating disorders (ED). I quickly became determined to prove that I had the discipline to become a great skater.

When I lost weight rapidly, everyone around me noticed. Where I had felt mediocre before, friends, acquaintances, and skating parents complimented me and asked me for advice. I even was allowed to skip our coach's mandatory weekly weigh-ins. All the positive attention fed my ED, and life circumstances accelerated my freefall.

In the spring of my freshman year of high school—years before cell phones—and just as I was beginning with ED, I lost touch with my school friends. I had missed a few days of school for a competition, a couple more for being sick, more for an emergency foot surgery, and then came spring break. It was close to one month of complete isolation, and I slipped into a dark place of hyper-independence fueled by fear, anxiety, and perfectionism.

Later, when I asked my school friends why they hadn't called to check on me, they all said they had thought I was skating. This is a common problem for young athletes in sports or activities that aren't school affiliated, particularly individual sports. I could have reached out to my friends, but my angsty fourteen-year-old self just wanted someone to miss me.

At the same time ED and anxiety were taking hold, my skating improved drastically. Sometimes, performance initially improves when athletes begin the spiral into disordered eating, and my experience was no exception. Since I was skating so well and had little to no friend engagement at school, I chose to transfer schools to make the commute easier.

Being in a new school allowed me to become even more introverted and focus solely on my schoolwork, weight, and skating. My mom taught at my new school, so I also felt many additional non-academic pressures there. It was a perfect storm.

Although my grades were near perfect and my skating was the best it had ever been, my mom was concerned about my mindset and health because I had stopped menstruating, so she took me to several different doctors. Whereas before doctors had told me to eat low-fat because of my genetically high cholesterol, now they were suggesting that I was too thin, yet not sick enough for medical intervention.

However, the more anyone mentioned my weight, the angrier and more determined I became to be the best at being thin. Perfectionism has long been documented as linked to eating disorders, which is why it is so common among high-level athletes and athletes in aesthetic sports, such as figure skating, gymnastics, and artistic swimming.

Restricting food and recreation gave me a sense of control during my teen years, and I was in overdrive to be the best. Anything less was a total failure and meant that I, too, was a failure.

I wish now that someone had shaken me and said, "Life is not a competition. You are already enough."

Ultimately, neither the commute nor the financial commitment was sustainable for my family. I didn't understand why, but kids never truly understand the details of parental sacrifice until much later. Bad genetics and the stress of our schedule caused my mom to have a heart attack. Thankfully, she fully recovered, but I knew we had to make some changes.

So, I chose to skate less and focus more on school and the college application process.

While figure skating is still not an NCAA sport, many universities currently offer skating as a club activity with opportunities for skaters of all levels to continue skating and competing in a friendly, supportive atmosphere. Twenty-five years ago, though, that option did not yet exist. Nevertheless, I wasn't willing to give up skating completely, so I chose a school that had a private rink somewhat nearby.

In the end, skating in college proved to be logistically difficult, but Butler University was the right choice for me. I received a good amount of academic scholarship money, an incredible liberal arts education (English and Spanish), and had a world of possibilities open to me through Butler's affordable study abroad program.

Although I was skating less than ever before, I still held tight to my athletic identity. I showed up at the rink for early morning practice, and I wore my sacrifice like a badge of honor. I had a great suitemate and a boyfriend from church who attended school in Kentucky, so I had my space but also phone support when needed. I managed to keep my ED quiet, and I finally started menstruating again. I even earned a 4.0 GPA and passed some skating skill level tests.

Sophomore year was a different game, though. As a resident assistant, I lived alone and was required to be on call many nights and weekends. I was still working to pay for skating but simply couldn't make it to the rink. Work, family illness, and religious trauma took over, and the ED came back in formidable ways.

Now I understand that I was dealing with years of toxic teachings and struggling with the identity loss that many young athletes go through after retirement. At the time, though, I thought I was just flawed. Everyone else seemed to be having fun, and I was lost.

Introverts recharge and recover by being alone, but too much alone time only leads to isolation and depression, and my depression had been brewing for years. Even if it runs counter to their nature, an athlete who is rebuilding their identity must try new things and seek out friends and community.

As I had always been a bit of a loner, I struggled with finding new friendships that clicked, and, honestly, I didn't have the energy or skills to try. I had no idea how to have fun and relax because ED and my church had so many rules about what were considered "safe" social activities. So, as usual, I poured myself into work and school. It's what I knew, and just as I learned with skating, I thought that if I were good enough, I would be accepted and happy.

We spend our whole lives as athletes being told to plan for the future, train for the goal, work hard for the next event, study hard to get scholarships, etc. Then, when things get tough, we're advised to "take things one step at a time." Unlearning a lifetime of athletic mental conditioning can take years (or decades), and for me, it certainly did.

I didn't have any guidance in navigating the after-sports transition. In fact, I think only one friend knew what I was going through that year. He was a former gymnast going through the same sort of identity and mental health issues, minus the ED.

I kept myself together on the outside, but alone in my room, I fell apart a little more each day under the weight of expectations from church, school, work, family, and myself. Deep down, I knew my personal path to healing was in creating space for myself. Being away at school hadn't provided enough distance, so I knew I needed to study abroad. My parents must have known I needed that, too, and I am so grateful that they supported that path for me.

I felt at home the minute I arrived in Sevilla, Spain for my year abroad. Making friends with the other students was fairly easy because we bonded over our shared fear, excitement, and cross-cultural observations. My new friends said they felt like they were in a dream, but I felt like I was awake for the first time ever.

I dove into life head-on because I saw a new world of possibilities, and I felt free. Best of all, the closest skating rink was a twelve-hour train ride away, so I had the real space away from skating that I needed.

During my time away, I fell in love with a boy from Colombia who had briefly attended my high school. We had met when I was tutoring ESL during my free period, and our friendship was unique. It felt minor back then, but we kept randomly coming back into contact with each other over the next few years.

He saw me in a way no one else had before, and I felt connected to him as I did to skating. He supported me unconditionally while I was in Spain, calling every Sunday to keep me feeling connected, talking me through the bouts of homesickness, and sharing our understanding of Spanish friends. I had found a new identity as someone who felt at home in two countries.

When I returned home for the summer, I thought the Colombian boy and I would be a couple, but he had other plans with other girls. I went back to Butler for senior year, and we kept in touch almost daily, even though he had broken off our relationship. He introduced me to his parents who had just immigrated from Colombia, and he made me feel special while simultaneously making me feel miserable.

I thought that, if I tried hard enough to be what everyone wanted, we would get back together. Walking away from him was like breaking up with skating all over again, and I chose to go to graduate school in Arizona to give myself new adventures far away.

At Arizona State I obtained a Master of Spanish Linguistics, with a focus on second language acquisition. The program was intense and exhilarating. I began teaching university Spanish right away and spent every waking hour with the same incredible people, many of whom are still my dearest friends today. I needed some variety from working, studying, and socializing with the same people though , so I decided to try coaching a Learn-to-Skate class or two.

When I went to the nearest skating rink to inquire about coaching, I ran into a friend I had skated with years before in Indiana. She was the connection I needed, and I was hired right away to begin coaching. I wanted to give skating another try.

As I began coaching, I found a community of welcoming colleagues and I rediscovered the joy of skating. Soon, I realized that coaching was more financially lucrative than being a teaching assistant, or even an adjunct professor, so I started coaching more and more as I worked toward my master's.

The honeymoon period in academia ended, too, as department politics drove several of my friends away from teaching. I immersed myself in skating again, and I decided to write my thesis on the language of instruction, creating a taxonomy of commands used in figure skating.

When I had studied in Sevilla in 1996, few people there had even heard of ice-skating rinks. In the year 2000, though, the internet was coming to life, and I found an online Spanish-language skating magazine that gave me contact information for several Spanish skating clubs. In 2001, I visited some of those clubs to collect data for my thesis. One of those clubs asked me to stay and work for them.

They wanted me to run their competitive skating club plus the municipal skating school in exchange for a decent salary, accommodations, use of a car, and a work visa. I had no written contract, just email exchanges with the club president pleading with me to help them rebuild their program. On paper, it was my dream job combining the two things I loved most—skating and Spain—and I was young and naive enough to take it.

Immediately after defending my MA thesis, I moved to Madrid, full of excitement and hope. I lived in a mansion with a very nice skating family and had use of one of their cars. I didn't even need to pay for food, and they invited me out to different places around town. However, the work situation was not as I had envisioned.

The club's previous coach was still at the rink giving me the evil eye and making me feel uncomfortable. Additionally, she was still under contract with the rink for six more months, so I would only be paid half of what was promised until then. I was paying off student loans and a credit card bill in the States, so panic and resentment hit me fast.

A couple of months later, the family that I lived with decided to move to Switzerland and took their car with them. I moved in with some friends of theirs that had nothing to do with skating—a nice family of expats who had kids my age living in the States.

They felt sorry for me, and they needed a house sitter for part of the summer, so the arrangement worked well. The club president lent me a car, but it was soon stolen from the rink parking lot, and I ended up without transportation.

In Spain, public transportation is quite good for certain areas, but the area in which I was living was for expats and wealthier families, so bus and train access were time-consuming and pricey. A few months later, that family also moved out of the country, and one of the hockey coaches and I moved into an apartment owned by the grandparent of a skater.

Commuting was easier from that apartment, and I truly enjoyed having my own space. I was now being paid in full, working half for the rink and half for the club, but now I would have to pay for rent and some utilities in addition to transportation. My resentment toward the skating club continued to build.

Around the same time, the situation at the club began to deteriorate. One of my colleagues and I didn't get along. She felt she should have gotten my job, and the parents thought I should be working miracles with their children. I struggled to take control of the situation because I didn't want to make uninformed decisions, and there was no information available.

The Spanish skating federation did not have a rulebook or a website, and the officials in charge ran the federation like a private insider's club where I was most certainly the outsider. I thought about leaving the club and only working for the rink, where I was experiencing loads of success building the program and working with the facility manager, but the work visa hadn't come through yet.

I was still being paid in cash, and, therefore, had no protections afforded to workers under contract. I was twenty-five and undocumented, too afraid to tell my parents how broke I was, or how tense the work environment was, and too stubborn and embarrassed to admit that my dream of working abroad was a flop.

Eventually, I burned out and quit my job with the club, which put me right back to earning half of the planned salary. I was free from a toxic environment, but now I was worse off financially than at the start because I had to pay rent and transportation out of half-pay. That situation was not sustainable, of course, and I felt I had to return to the US.

I felt duped. I blamed myself for not knowing better than to buy into empty promises, and I blamed the club president for misleading me and failing to look out for me once I got there. While I was deep in the blame game and figuring out my next steps, my Colombian boyfriend reappeared via a 4:00 am phone call.

I instantly recognized the voice, even though it had been five years since we had spoken. He missed me and wanted me to come back to Louisville. I declined, but we began a long-distance romance that filled me with a hope like I had never felt before.

Just as he did when I was in Spain the first time, he supported me unconditionally. He job-searched with me, printed resumes, and delivered them for me, and believed in my potential and worth in a way that I did not. I thought I had regained a portion of my identity.

I did end up moving back to Louisville (which finally had a new rink) in mid-2003, and the Colombian disappointed me again. The next few years were a blur of seventy to eighty-hour work weeks and an on-again-off-again toxic relationship. I taught Spanish at several universities in Louisville, volunteered as skating club president, took over the role of the artistic director, coached every hour possible, and managed to fit in a bit of travel abroad. I bought my own condo, paid off student loans, got health insurance, bought a new car, adopted a cat, and did all the responsible adult things.

I dedicated countless hours to studying how to be the best coach possible, and I passed many coaching certification exams. I was determined to prove that Louisville could have what we didn't have growing up here—quality programming and high-level skaters—and determined to fit in within a sport where I hadn't before.

A small, dedicated team of coaches and club volunteers worked unimaginable hours and built a program that ultimately led to several national medals in singles, pairs, dance, and synchronized skating. Finally, the Colombian and I broke it off for good.

As the successes came, so did the failures. Our club had tried to create a culture of excellence, which was code for toxic clique culture. The competition-driven environment excluded many young skaters, and those that were included knew they were always vying for a space at the top of the imaginary totem pole.

This was the daily training environment, and no one was safe except the most recreational. When I split philosophically from the other coaches, working together as a team became unbearable, and many high-level skaters left our club, and the sport, traumatized. There were no clear grievances or complaints for me to file for unethical behavior or emotional abuse, but the evidence was all around me.

Eventually, a lifetime of perfectionism, striving, people-pleasing, feelings of inadequacy, betrayals, and toxic relationships took their toll on my physical and mental health. In 2013, I saw a Groupon for a local non-profit yoga school, and just as my gut told me I had to go to Spain in 1996, my gut sent me to practice yoga. Showing up to the mat every day free of expectations was the single most transformative experience I had ever had.

The healing journey is not a straight path, and I've had many bumps and curves along the way. What is undoubtedly true is that the more focused I am on yoga, the clearer my head is, the less attached to outcomes I am, and the more effective teacher I am. With my mind clear and my heart unattached to outcomes, I became free to be the best version of myself.

When you learn to take things one day at a time and observe instead of reacting, beautiful paths open for you. I began to apply yoga to my coaching, met someone new, got married, became a parent, started dabbling in other sports purely for enjoyment, and began to heal.

I don't love skating now—striving too hard for too long led me to burnout. However, I do love the people I've helped and connected with along the way, and I'm grateful for the many positive lessons and experiences I've had.

At this moment, US Figure Skating says they are dealing with the layers of abuse that occur in the sport, and maybe they are trying, but the reality is that high-level sports are abusive by nature. Emotional abuse and toxic environments are too often tolerated because they are hard to prove.

> "
> When you learn to take things one day at a time and observe instead of reacting, beautiful paths open for you.
> "

One of my main defects has always been putting people I love and admire on pedestals, expecting too much from them, and believing too little in myself. In the end, mentors, friends, and boyfriends were doomed to disappoint me because they were human. It's much easier to paint a picture as black and white and blame others for our circumstances and our feelings.

Obviously, in many circumstances, there is very clear wrongdoing and abuse that needs to be addressed punitively. In many other instances, however, it's most helpful to recognize that we are all humans living through the lens of our traumas and our life teachings. With this in mind, we should know that only education and compassion can help make lasting change.

We must recognize toxic and harmful behaviors in sport (and society) for what they are, learn the lessons we are meant to learn, and pass along the knowledge gained. I have found yoga to be the most helpful teacher of all.

When Covid-19 forced a three-month shutdown of our rink in early 2020, I realized that the lasting trauma I experienced from toxic thought processes and environments ran deeper than I had imagined. Science now shows that even micro-traumas have lasting effects on our nervous system, which can lead to long-term health issues. The deeper I go in my yoga practice, the more I understand just how important a balanced nervous system is to our overall health.

Because of this, I know I don't want to coach in the same skating world I grew up in, or the one I coached in pre-Covid. I want to be a part of the solution to the mental health crisis in skating (and sports, in general) by helping this generation learn to follow their own path, maintain a strong sense of identity beyond sports, and build resiliency. No one should have to lose themselves in their efforts to succeed in the sport.

The Skating Yogi is an online space I founded that connects athletes of different ages and sports through yoga, mindfulness, and community. We use asana (physical postures), breathwork, meditation, journal prompts, and discussion to help member athletes heal from burnout, manage anxiety, regain self-confidence, learn to follow their individual paths, and reclaim their authentic identities.

For many years I tried to prove that I was worthy enough and that I belonged in the social and skating circles where I was trying to be. Those efforts were fruitless, as they always are. My mission now is not to prove anything to anyone, but rather to show athletes that they are worth more than their accomplishments and that there is no better place to belong than within themselves.

ABOUT SARAH

Sarah Neal is a master-rated figure skating coach, yoga teacher, traveler, adjunct professor, lover of Spain and the Spanish language, almost-vegan, and bookworm. Born into a family of teachers, she fell in love with skating at an early age and always wanted to make skating her career. After a problematic relationship with the sport, compulsive perfectionism, and an eating disorder, she stopped competing to focus on college and trying to build a new identity.

Eventually, the search led her to study abroad in Spain, where she found herself at home for the first time in many years. During graduate school for Spanish linguistics, she decided to rewrite her skating story and return to the sport to coach.

It wasn't until beginning a consistent yoga practice in 2013 that she began to heal and feel comfortable in her own skin after a lifetime of anxiety, depression, and disordered eating. Connecting with the breath and slowing down to be present on the mat was the greatest, most powerful transformation she had ever experienced.

Now, Sarah takes over four decades of athletic experience and two decades of teaching, coaching, directing, programming, and life experience to help former and current athletes find peace on the mat and within themselves.

She helps them connect their breath and awareness to their bodies, minds, and spirits, so they can move beyond their athletic conditioning to build healthier relationships with themselves and step into new chapters of their lives.

Chapter 11

SELF-KNOWLEDGE IS THE KEY TO SUSTAINABLE SUCCESS BY CHLOE MALESKI

I realized early on that I wanted to excel in sports. Growing up in New England, athletics seemed to be the most important form of entertainment, and even an obsession for most people around me. We cold, gritty, New Englanders, took pride in our Patriots, Red Sox, Bruins, and Celtics. They were the closest thing we had to superheroes, as far as I was concerned.

I later learned that providing entertainment was not an elite athlete's sole contribution to the people around them. It is also the athlete's mindset that draws others to them: the mental toughness, perseverance, and unwavering dedication to show up every single day to train and compete.

I wanted to be a part of this. I wanted to be looked up to, respected, and legendary. Sports seemed like the avenue to achieve this, so I made it my goal to excel at a sport that would propel me forward, rather than one I necessarily loved.

I grew up with three brothers who all played sports in some capacity. I was always trying to prove that I could be as good (or better) than they were as athletes. I don't think anyone knew that this was part of my motivation, but I sure did. It's not that my relationships with my brothers was bad, in fact, it was always pretty good.

However, being a female athlete, they never saw me as competition; I only saw them as competition. It can get tiring playing games that you weren't even invited to.

I remember a time in fifth grade when I came home from school, and I was so excited to tell my dad how I had beaten all the boys at arm wrestling.

He told me, "That's great, but you know you're not always going to be stronger than the boys."

I cried for an hour in my bedroom. What he said had made so sad, and I thought it was so unfair. Why was it that I could work twice as hard as them, and not be stronger just because I was a female?

This also made me realize that all the teams I watched and admired were comprised of men. I recognized then and there that I never wanted to be a professional female athlete, I wanted to be a professional male athlete. I wanted the confidence, legendary status, and high income that male athletes possessed.

At the time, the only popular female athlete I knew of was Olympic gold medalist, Mia Hamm, and she was still being paid a fraction of what male athletes on the same level were making.

My long-term goal was to shine in sports and try to get a scholarship at a respected college that would get me out of my small town. In my mind, running was the best avenue to do this. The seed had been planted in elementary school. I ran the fastest mile for the boys and girls, then went on to middle school and won the cross-country state championship.

I should add that, at this point, I started to put a lot of pressure on myself. Winning was fun, but if I didn't win, I did not enjoy running. By the time I got to high school, I was deep in the consideration of whether I wanted to continue running cross-country or play soccer since they were both fall sports. The athletic director ended up making an exception for me, and I was allowed to play soccer while competing in the races for cross-country. I was the first female athlete to participate in two sports in one season.

I played basketball in the winter, and ran track in the spring, as well. By my junior year, I was getting very intense and focused on running. I gave up soccer, and even though I continued to play basketball in the winter, I would get up at 5:00 am before school to run. Sometimes, it was negative seventeen degrees outside, but I knew my determination and consistency would get me places. I'll never forget the day I had to miss the first half of school because my legs were numb from my morning run.

As time went on and I saw more success in running, I also realized it was less of a burden for my family than other sports had been. I didn't have to pay for equipment (besides sneakers), unlike my brothers, who were playing sports such as hockey and lacrosse. These included costs of ice time, tons of equipment, and so on. I also didn't need a ride to practices and tournaments. I could run anywhere.

In retrospect, I knew that my parents didn't have a plethora of resources for four kids to play sports, and I didn't want to be too much of a financial burden. I just committed to running, despite the fact that I disliked it. It perpetuated the pressure I constantly put on myself to succeed. In track, you can't pass the ball to anyone, and you can't depend on the rest of the team to carry you. You either win, or you don't, and it all hangs on your performance.

Here's what I did like about it, though. Running was the sport where I felt I had the most control. John Wooden's quote sums it up best: "Don't let the things you cannot do interfere with the things you can."

Running was where I felt I had the most jurisdiction over what I could do. My effort was immediately actualized. The harder I worked, the further I went, the faster I got, and the more I won. Mission accomplished. It was so rewarding. I loved the affirmations I was getting from my family, friends, and community by running fast and winning. I felt important and loved.

Despite this, the fact of the matter was that I hated running. Simply put, it hurts! Running as an athlete requires you to push yourself to your absolute limits and test the boundaries of your physical capabilities. I loved to win, but to race and run, not so much.

However, I was getting so much validation from the outside world that I was not brave enough to walk away from it. I was in the newspaper almost every day, and I was a hometown hero and Gatorade athlete of the year for New Hampshire. Most importantly, I felt like my parents and friends loved and respected me more because I was excelling in the sport.

This was a slippery slope to relying on the outside world for validation of my self-worth early on in life. In fact, I still catch myself doing this at times. My coping mechanism when I feel sad, isolated, left out, or not good enough is to excel and achieve.

This makes me feel worthy and respected because results don't lie. If I can prove to myself and the world that I can do something, how could they not love me? And even if they don't, I feel satisfied with my own discipline and hard work. However, this often only serves to create a bigger chip on my shoulder. It's something I still have to keep in check, and as a Forever Athlete, I'm exploring this and working on it daily.

You might be wondering what it means to be a Forever Athlete. It means to ask questions of yourself; to continue to explore yourself and build that self-knowledge. The more you know yourself, the more peace you can have in your life. Self-knowledge is the root of all happiness if you ask me, and the way to achieve this is to continue with curiosity in every part of your life.

I do this by showing up for myself on a consistent basis and keeping my focus on personal development and growth. It is an ongoing practice of asking myself pointed questions about my intentions and deciphering my motivation for my actions so that I can continue to move forward toward my goals. Sometimes it feels like the effort isn't paying off, but those moments of struggle have the best potential for a breakthrough.

Through my experience and self-knowledge, I have realized that sports are also an avenue of coping, just in a more socially acceptable way. Just as drugs or alcohol provide an escape from reality, so does running for an athlete with a perfectionist mindset.

> "
> Self-knowledge is the root of all happiness if you ask me, and the way to achieve this is to continue with curiosity in every part of your life.
> "

Many of my runner friends need to get their torturous workout or long run in before they can feel good about themselves for the day. It is a way to get socially acceptable "high," to punish themselves for any perceived shortcomings, or make up for what they might perceive as a failure in another area of their life.

Society sees it as a product of discipline and hard work, but is running our bodies to the ground in order to feel good about ourselves really beneficial? I would recommend that everyone, before competing in a sport, think deeply about why they are doing it. Being self-aware is the first step of being a Forever Athlete. Self-awareness allows you to show up where it counts for yourself and others.

Many of us go through the motions of life without truly knowing the reason behind what we do. Often, these motivators are external and based purely on the people and events around us. By allowing yourself to be internally motivated, you can act in a way that aligns with your core values and pushes you toward the things you want to accomplish.

I have always been frustrated with the perception that athletes are inherently healthy simply because they are active. Movement is usually the first thing that a therapist prescribes when working with an anxious or depressed client. However, they might not realize the pressure and other challenges that come along with the movement in the sport itself. We have seen repeatedly the cost of the high pressure put on professional athletes, leaving them mentally shot.

Naomi Osaka and Simone Biles are two notable athletes who respectably stepped away from the French Open and the Olympics. Both of them were favorites to win, but they chose not to compete for the sake of their mental health and wellbeing. This was met with lots of backlash from the press.

However, if Osaka or Biles had harmed themselves, or started engaging in self-destructive behavior as a result of their mental state, there would be a public outcry for more empathy regarding elite athletes, and the demand to let them take time off when needed.

When you reach a higher level of sport, it seems that everyone is your biggest fan, while simultaneously waiting to watch you fall. This pressure can feel insurmountable. Add social media and public exposure into the mix, and things can really look bleak and overwhelming.

It would have been easy for Osaka or Biles to react in a negative way. Can you relate to this? When you feel hurt, disrespected, or unloved it is natural to want to retaliate.

Revenge looks different for everyone, but I can tell you this; taking that step will only hurt you more. For example, my taking revenge on others, by excelling and overachieving, only created a reliance on outside validation, which ultimately led to low self-esteem. If your preferred revenge is to fight back, you will only get charged, expelled, or whatever the punishment might be. Do you see where I'm getting here? Revenge has the biggest negative impact on the person distributing it.

So, what's the best way to cope? I believe the answer is self-awareness, and the ability to exhibit love and kindness toward yourself through these painful situations. This is the paradox of being an athlete. You have to find the balance between being competitive and great, while also being a good human and keeping perspective. It's these intrinsic feelings and values that will propel you the furthest, and keep you from getting burned out mentally and emotionally.

The next step to be a Forever Athlete is taking action. Do you have any negative thought patterns that you maintain in your own life, whether in your sport or outside of it? If you're human, you most likely do. It's important to work every day on reversing these negative thought patterns and finding boundaries to keep yourself accountable when it comes to being mentally healthy.

Start with just one negative thought that comes up often and reframe it. For example, "I'm not strong enough," could change to, "I'm getting stronger every day."

Find a new way to look at these perceived shortcomings, and practice thinking about them in a constructive light. Be consistent and practice these mental skills daily, just like you would practice your free throw. These habits will allow you to flourish mentally, and therefore better support your physical endeavors as an athlete.

If you go into a college or professional team's locker room, not much is going to change physically day-to-day. What really sets athletes apart is their mental state. I would, however, like to mention that people can be high performers in their sport and be mentally unhealthy.

I believe this is unsustainable, and at some point, that person will break. Self-awareness, healthy boundaries, and forming habits are key to achieving continued success and health. When I say health, that encapsulates everything: mental health, physical health, financial health, etc.

Recently in therapy, I had a breakthrough, in which I visualized my parents at the starting line of one of my middle school races. They were telling me they would still love me if I didn't run. This visualization was so potent that it brought me to tears. It was so powerful, as I would get overwhelmingly nervous for these races as an eleven-year-old. I felt my parents knew I hated it, but they never asked me about it. Now, I wish they had asked questions. As an adult, I know that most parents are trying to do their best, but it's my responsibility to ask myself questions as well.

Now, when I move my body, I do it with curiosity. I do it as an expression of myself. I do it intentionally. As a coach, I work with athletes on the mental side of sports. I am always asking questions of my athletes about their *why*. What keeps them showing up? I encourage them to visualize and express their day-to-day experiences with their sport. In short, I support them in staying as connected to their mind and body as possible.

Being a Forever Athlete means working every day to find that balance. To find your flow, the sweet spot where you can perform at your best while still being challenged. You are listening to your body, heart, and soul.

Through my education, experience as an athlete, and work with my clients, I have come up with a few mental tools you can utilize in your endeavor to be a Forever Athlete.

Core Values: How often do you hear people say they are stressed? Probably a lot. What is the feeling of stress? It is the feeling of not knowing your core values, and therefore being pulled in two directions. An example is "I need to get shots (basketball) up, but I want to go to this party to see my friend." As soon as you choose to get shots up or go to the party, the stress is gone because you have made the decision.

Use the worksheet below to figure out what your core values are!

VIVID *vision* VALUES SHEET

Abundance	Love	Family	Flexibility
Daring	Reliability	Performance	Security
Intuition	Appreciation	Stability	Growth
Acceptance	Enthusiasm	Caring	Safety
Decisiveness	Loyalty	Friendships	Usefulness
Joy	Resilience	Personal	Collaboration
Proactivity	Resourcefulness	Development	Health
Achievement	Attractiveness	Success	Professionalism
Dedication	Making a Difference	Challenge	Contribution
Kindness	Autonomy	Flexibility	Humility
Professionalism	Ethics	Proactive	Warmth
Advancement	Mindfulness	Charity	Creativity
Dependability	Excellence	Freedom	Credibility
Knowledge	Balance	Cleverness	Wealth
Punctuality	Responsibility	Generosity	Community
Adventure	Expressiveness	Risk Taking	Grace
Diversity	Motivation	Trustworthiness	Playfulness
Leadership	Preparedness	Commitment	Welk-being
Recognition	Responsiveness	Open-mindedness	Independence
Advocacy	Being the Best	Originality	Curiosity
Empathy	Optimism	Selflessness	Popularity
Learning	Security	Fairness	Wisdom
Relationships	Benevolence	Passion	Power
Ambition	Simplicity	Service	Innovation
Encouragement	Calmness	Happiness	Intelligence

Step 1: Determine your values: Circle all values that resonate with you.

Step 2: Identify your strengths and write them down.

Step 3: List the things you are passionate about.

Step 4: Group all similar values together. Try to get down to your top five!)

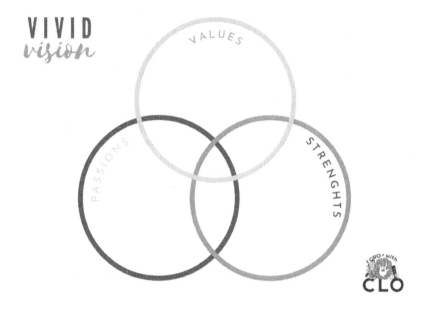

Now, you can use this self-knowledge to help guide you. You can feel confident with the decisions you make, knowing you put the time and effort into getting to know yourself and what's most important to you. If you are still a bit stuck here, write down three people you admire most, and the notable qualities they have. See which ones align with the top values that you wrote down previously.

Stoplight: This is a mindfulness tool. Meditation is hard for many, but this is a way to get back to the present moment during practice or a game. When you find yourself overwhelmed or unable to ground yourself, you have been caught at a red light. Your goal is to change your thinking and get back in touch with the moment.

When this happens to you, try visualizing the red, yellow, and green glow of a stoplight.

Red Light: You are trapped by your negative thoughts. *That play was awful, my legs hurt, it's too hot out.* Whatever the thought may be, it is keeping you from performing at your best.

Yellow Light: In order to snap out of it, you need to connect to something *real*. Feel the sweat dripping down your forehead, run your cleats over the grass, or focus on the sound of your breath. Don't allow those negative thoughts to pull you out of the moment.

Green Light: Reframe your thoughts in a positive way: *I crushed that last play, I feel great, I've got this!*

The goal of this exercise is to get out of our own way. Red lights are self-destructive and often lead to a spiral of negative thoughts. Do not force yourself to green light but focus on getting back to something real (yellow light) and physical. This helps us realize that we are not controlled by our thoughts. Eventually, you may get to the green, but the exercise is meant to focus on getting back to the present moment, rather than following those negative thoughts.

Feedback, Not Failure: We all make mistakes but reframing them as feedback rather than failures is a game-changer. Develop a ritual you can use to move on to the next play. Tell yourself you will learn from it afterward, but right now your most important role is to be present.

For example, if you fumble, you can hit your helmet or brush your shoulder off to remind yourself to move on from the mistake. You will reflect and learn from that incident later when you have the time, but for now, the most important play is the current or next one, with no time to dwell on the past. Presence is power.

With these tools, you can begin to free yourself from the shackles of the negative thought processes which keep you from performing at your best. Each of them touches on grounding yourself in the current moment, reframing your thoughts, and, most importantly, being kind to yourself. Self-knowledge may be the key to success, but it is only by tending to your mental wellbeing that success will be sustainable.

Today, I am happy to say that I have finally fallen in love with running. I could never understand how I had gone from the exuberant fifth-grader who loved making great time on the mile, to an adult who hated running. Instead of giving it up completely, I began to incorporate other activities that I found fulfilling into my physical and mental wellness routine. I worked on maintaining a positive mindset, engaging in healthy relationships, and starting strength training.

Recently, I ran the Boston Marathon with a time of 3:04, and I intend to continue working on my overall wellbeing with all of the tools and methods I have shared with you in this chapter. Walking the talk, so to speak, is immensely important to me. I strive to utilize the methods and strategies I provide for my clients in my own life and turning my words into tangible improvements in performance is, in my mind, a large part of my identity as a Forever Athlete.

I call myself a Forever Athlete not because I will never give up sports (and I don't intend to!), but because the qualities, self-awareness, and life lessons that I have received throughout my athletic career will stay with me forever. I have learned to be internally motivated rather than externally motivated, and when faced with choices, I try to always consult my core values.

Does this reflect the person I aspire to show up as? What makes me happy? What value does this add to my life? How will this help me grow?

These are the questions you should be asking yourself, as well, especially if you are reaching the end or have already concluded your athletic career.

As an athlete, we already know that you have the strength, determination, and perseverance to excel in any field that you choose. The crucial part of this transition is making sure you are in touch with your mind, body, and core values so that you can take the best next step in your journey.

ABOUT CHLOE

Chloe Maleski is a mental performance coach with the goal of helping athletes grow into the best version of themselves and optimize their performance in a sustainable way.

Through visualization, mindfulness, stress management, and cognitive-behavioral performance, she helps athletes foster all parts of themselves in order to enhance, not only their athletic performance, but their overall wellbeing and lives!

She was a collegiate distance runner at Duke University with an underwhelming career during her time there. Since graduating, she continued to train, compete, and study all aspects of her experience in order to figure out what happened.

She graduated from Primal Health Coach Institute with her Master of Clinical Psychology, and became a certified personal trainer. Her education has helped bridge the gap between wellness and performance, and the importance of mind-body connection when performing at an elite level.

She would love to help you grow into the best athlete and person you can possibly be!

Connect with Chloe:
Website: www.growithclo.com
IG: @growithclo_
Twitter: @growithclo
LinkedIn: https://www.linkedin.com/in/chloemaleski/
Facebook: https://www.facebook.com/Gro-With-Clo-103258415201112

Chapter 12

FILL THE GAP
BY CODY ALLEN

In the year 1996, my mom was signing up her chubby five-year-old for whatever sport would take him. I played soccer, baseball, and I think we even tried karate back then. This seems to be the standard for many young boys.

Their parents put them into a sport to teach them the value of hard work, how to play well with others, and, in all honesty, to get a break from them for an hour or so. This might sound lighthearted, but, in reality, this is the foundation of not only building a better future athlete but also creating a more well-rounded individual in the long run.

I wouldn't say that I was born athletic by any means. There are those who are gifted, and those who aren't. I was probably somewhere between the two. With that being said, sports didn't come easy to me at first. I was what you called an MPR kid, which stands for "minimum plays required."

In other words, kids like me only played as much as the rules required us to because our parents paid for us to play city ball. Being eleven years old, or so, in Little League proved to be a great teaching lesson for me. I knew what it felt like to not be my best at something, and the only way to get rid of that feeling was to put in the work to become great.

At this young age, I was able to learn that hard work is the thing that will distance you from failure the most. Each strikeout, missed fly ball, or grounder between my legs was an opportunity to grow.

Looking back, I know that my drive, my athlete's mentality, and ambition to improve, is what made me different from the others—the ability to face adversity when you're not confident, when you're feeling down on yourself, or when everyone is looking at you and wondering why you don't just quit. That is what stays with you and makes you a Forever Athlete. That is what sets you apart from the rest.

Long story short, that MPR kid became one of the best all-stars in his region and excelled in the sport. It wasn't because I got more playing time but because I did what was necessary to change my situation.

Little league baseball was fun, of course, but I had bigger aspirations. I started playing organized football in high school. I still remember the first day of practice. The coach told everyone to line up for sprints with the position they wanted to play. I knew nothing about football, but I was five-foot-nine and 180 pounds.

I remembered that the Chargers were good at the time, and I had seen Antonio Gates catch a bunch of touchdowns. I thought I might like to do that, so I decided to run with the tight ends. Little did I know that this practice would probably be the most impactful in my life.

I still remember the moment I nervously lined up with the tight end group, heart racing and ready to do anything other than come in last place on our sprints.

I looked up to see the coach point at me, and, in front of the entire team, he said, "You're a big boy. You go run with the linemen."

I don't remember the coach that said that, but I'll never forget the feeling of embarrassment that pooled in the pit of my stomach.

I quickly put my head down and jogged over to the part of the line where the "big boys" were running in hopes that nobody saw me. This moment in my life was an opportunity I was blessed with.

I could either fold and let my emotions bring me down, or I could rise to the occasion and show the coach why I should be a tight end by kicking everyone's ass in the sprints. If I had chosen the first, I probably wouldn't be writing this. That day, I finished every sprint first or second on the entire team, beating out all the skinnier and, supposedly, faster kids on the team.

Immediately after practice, the coach told me I was going to be playing tailback for the team. That was amazing, except I had no idea what a tailback was. A day and a few Google searches later, I was ready to become the elite athlete I knew I could be.

> "
> Looking back, I know that my drive, my athlete's mentality, and ambition to improve, is what made me different from the others.
> "

From that point on, I was "Cody Allen the football player" to most. That's what people tend to do; we find something we're good at and become obsessed with it. We put all our focus and effort into it until it's woven into the fabric of our very being and identity. This inherent human quality is amazing and horrible all at the same time.

When it comes to athletics, most won't achieve the highest accolades, level of greatness, or even their full potential unless they are all-in on being successful. If you're not willing to put in the work, someone else will, and they'll beat you. This is a valuable lesson that must be learned if you want to be truly great at your sport.

Even with the maximum amount of effort, you will still experience failures and mishaps. That is where the upper echelon athletes thrive. When things get tough, you fail, or you're down, that's your opportunity to build on your weakness and come back even harder.

My athletic career, like most, had many peaks and valleys. My life, too, has had its share of highs and lows. I have been fired from jobs, broken up with, and made more mistakes than I can count. I'm human, and that's what we do. We live and learn.

I have also struggled with the fact that my birth father walked away from my family when I was six. I did not hear from him again until a few months after my twenty-ninth birthday. As a result, I have always felt the need to achieve accolades and seek approval from my elders in hopes of feeling worthy to them. Luckily, I have an amazing mother and stepfather to help me realize my value. But, at times in life, especially when you're young, some obstacles seem insurmountable.

Being an athlete prepared me for the challenges thrown at me. When I was knocked down, I was ready to come back with a vengeance.

My high school football career went from zero to one hundred as quickly as the ref could blow the whistle of my first snap. When I said that sports didn't come to me naturally, I wasn't talking about football. I quickly discovered that I was made for the sport, not just physically, but mentally as well.

In the game of football, they say you need to have a short-term memory. You need to be able to move on from the previous play immediately to get yourself ready for the next. I had always operated that way, and football gave me the opportunity to play on that strength.

A couple of years before football started, I played in the Little League All-Stars Regional Baseball Tournament. It was the semi-finals, and we were down by a run with a runner on second with two outs. I came up to bat. I had just about every nervous tick or feeling you could think of.

Two strikes went by, and I took a step out of the batter's box to collect myself. The past was the past, and I had to focus on the next pitch alone. On the very next pitch, I hit a double between the center and left fielder to tie the game. This was just one time I used that short-term memory to fuel a win for my team.

By year two I was a starter on varsity for football, and, from then on, I was receiving countless accolades for my quarterback and safety play. None were more valuable than the scholarship I received from California State University, Sacramento to play linebacker. This part of my story is important. I went from being a stand-out player at quarterback and safety to being a D1 AA linebacker, a much more physically demanding spot on the field.

When you're from a relatively small town in California like I am, people tend to prop you up for what you do on the field. When I transitioned to Sac State, I went from being highly touted and small-town-famous to being nobody. I was a small fish in a big pond.

When I went into my first fall camp, I was a talented, albeit cocky, recruit. My ego was running high, and I was coming off a two-year streak of being one of the best players in my region. I went into camp too confident, and I was quickly sobered up by the complex playbook, higher level of game speed, and violent play.

Just as life is full of success and happiness, it is also full of failures and doubts. How you react to these doubts will determine your success rate. The reason I make this point is that, at the time of going into my first camp, I felt like I had reached a high in my sports career only to be filled with self-doubt due to the new challenges that college football brought.

Often in life, business, and athletics, we are faced with decisions that force us to lean into the hard times and power through with resilience. That's exactly what I did. I studied the game day-in and day-out.

I learned the playbook front to back. Most importantly, I did the reps. When things get tough, and when we find that we aren't good at something, we tend to just back off and avoid doing that thing. But if that's the route you take, you'll never get better. I faced my deficiencies head-on, and only through challenging myself was I able to get better.

By the end of my freshman year, I was named Most Outstanding Scout Defensive MVP. This is important because where I started that first year and where I ended it were at opposite ends of the spectrum. But it was the hard work and dedication in between that got me there.

Everyone's athletic journey is different and similar at the same time. It's never easy, but it's always worth it. When it's all said and done, you've grown more as an individual than you could've ever imagined. This is the reason athletes excel in the business world after their sports careers have ended.

Once you're an athlete, you're always an athlete. No matter if it's on the court, the field, or behind a desk, the athletic mindset, the drive to improve your game and climb to the top of your team, is in you forever.

Everything I've touched on so far should be relatable to anyone who has made sports a long-term part of their life to some degree. The ups and downs are part of it. They're unavoidable, and, in many cases, they are welcomed. Now, I would like to focus on the biggest unspoken struggle that all athletes will inevitably face: what do you do when your career is over?

Your athletic career is a relatively small percentage of your life, yet it consumes so much of who you are as an individual. We will forever identify as the athlete we once were, and, for some, that is an issue. What are we supposed to do when the game we played no longer has a spot on the roster for us?

I faced this circumstance when my collegiate career ended. I had a decision to make: chase my dreams of going pro in the NFL or start my "adult" career. Given my injury history, and the fact that I thought I might not be good enough, I chose to dive into the workforce.

What did that look like for me? I got into banking. That's the smart thing to do, right? Chase money and build a good life. What I didn't realize is that I would find it nearly impossible to have the same vigor and put forth the same level of effort toward a desk job as I did on the gridiron.

A lot of football players, myself included, don't know what to do athletically after our careers are over. My advice to you is to find something you love that you can still do competitively as that will ignite the fire inside you that is dying to burn. Outside of your nine-to-five, you need to find that athletic thing to do with your body because that was the tool you used to get you to the success you found to this point.

Without it, the days lull by. I joined every city flag football, softball, and functional training team I could find to ensure that I still was able to push myself to the level I wanted to. People are extremely intricate and unique. But one thing that seems to be common amongst every person is having a desire for self-worth and self-development in one way or another.

When I jumped back into athletics, I found that I saw improvements in all aspects of my life, career, and personal alike. The workdays didn't seem so bad when I had something to look forward to. The zest I'd once had for life came back.

Continuing to play sports in some fashion feeds the soul of an athlete the same way that an artist will paint to feed theirs. Sure, I was playing against people who had never touched a pro field, but returning to your sport and nurturing your competitive nature is something that feeds your soul. To this day, you can still catch me playing in some sort of league a few times a week.

It was extremely important for me to continue to work on my physical fitness and health. Doing so allows you to feel that familiar sense of athletic worth. While your body permits, don't take it for granted. Setting and achieving goals is essential for overall happiness. Sports allow you to grow, learn, fail, and conquer what you may not have thought you could.

Continuing to test me and create sustainable relationships through team sports has been instrumental in my growth as an adult. It may seem like a dumb game, but it's anything but that. The correlation between my health, wellness, and happiness is strong. I feel that I'm a better friend, peer, and overall person in society when I feel healthy. This plays a massive role in your mental health and confidence, as well. These elements directly correlate to the success you'll ultimately be able to find in life.

That being said, success looks different for everyone. It could be a big house and a fancy car, or it might be forging real and sustainable relationships with those you love. It might be everything in between. But I am a firm believer that former and current athletes have a significant competitive advantage when entering the business world.

I often brought the same attitude to the office that I once did on the football field. I found a tenacity to want to be the best and gave an effort second to none. This helped me surpass my peers, purely based on merit. It's vital that you never lose that edge. As an athlete, you need to be pushed. Often, that push needs to come from within.

I can tell you firsthand that working a nine-to-five can get dull quickly. It was only a few years before I felt myself becoming bored with the monotony of corporate America. So, after finding success within the finance space via promotions and accolades, I moved on. When you start to lose that edge, you need to find something to sharpen the sword.

While working in finance and banking, I found myself too often saying, "I could do that better," when speaking about someone's business.

Did I know if I could actually do it better? Of course not. But, as an athlete, we often set the goalposts just out of reach so that we take the steps necessary to reach them.

We've all heard the saying: "Push yourself outside of your comfort zone."

That's what I needed to do, and I did.

I jumped into digital marketing, a field I was not familiar with, but one that seemed to be taking over every media outlet. In my mind, marketing is sales, and I knew how to sell because I'd been selling myself as an athletic prospect for years. I didn't know much about the intricacies of the business, but I did know there was money to be made, and, if others were doing it, I could too. That's the edge I'm talking about. You challenge yourself, and the things you're doing suddenly have a new sense of worth.

Being your own boss is one of the hardest things a person will ever do. But, as an athlete, I did what we do best, and I bet on myself. When you're a business owner, your successes and failures ultimately fall on your shoulders.

I love that, and I feed off of it. Getting into the digital space was a tough nut to crack and will always come with new hardships, but the things that made me a great athlete, teammate, and eventual coach helped me find success within the space.

Despite the natural talent that many athletes possess, the truth is that nobody is born knowing how to play a particular sport. There is a learning curve for everyone, and without being a meticulous student of the game, you'll never reach your full potential. I used my diligent study techniques taken from the game film room to become a student of the digital marketing space, learning the ins, outs, and potential pitfalls of the industry.

Something that playing quarterback and middle linebacker taught me was how to look at the bigger picture by knowing every detail. Being the captain and play-caller of the offense and defense means that you need to know what every person is doing on every single play. This is very similar to the role of a business owner.

Successful athletes possess a trait that most people don't have. They're accountable. You can't exactly *fake it till you make it* on the field. If you're not doing your job, then you not only let yourself down but your teammates as well. In order to mitigate your risk of exposure to failure, you work your ass off and shore up your game. The business world is about being innovative, reliable, and a good partner when needed. Without sounding too cliché, you need to embrace the grind because that's where winners are made.

Just like when I started college football, I went from what I thought was the top to the bottom. Entering a new field in which I had no experience or knowledge stripped me of my confidence and filled me with self-doubt. That's what it's like to start a business after leaving an industry you're successful in. I was all too familiar with the feeling and knew that, even with the doubts, I could prevail just as I had before.

A best practice to make you disciplined in your approach to success is to remember that feeling in the pit of your stomach when you fail—that gut-wrenching urge to just give up.

You know that it goes away when you bounce back and start to see the fruits of your hard labor. Most people are so afraid of that feeling because they fear it will never go away. I'm here to tell you what you already know. The only way that feeling wins is if you give in and give up.

Athletes are constantly thrown into the fire and put under stress while being expected to perform at their peak levels. This is another reason why athletes prevail in the business world. Every day you wake up, it seems like there is another fire to put out or danger ahead.

Making clear and sound decisions while dealing with those pressures makes for one success after the other. Stress and competition bring out the best in us. If you can thrive under those conditions, you can thrive in the business world. Most athletes have been doing that their entire lives.

The biggest advantage athletes have had over the years in finding success has been their discipline. Discipline has the biggest effect on your ability to reach sustainable success. Take note of the word sustainable here; the goal for success is longevity. Anyone can get lucky once or twice, but being disciplined will yield repeated success you can build on.

All of these reasons are why I hire athletes and why athletes want to do business with me. Being disciplined is an admirable quality that athletes learn early, but it is a quality that gets tested every day in our careers.

How many times has a coach yelled, "Run through the line!" or "Finish the rep!" during conditioning? Does that extra rep really make you that much stronger, faster, or in better shape? In short, no. But it does give you the mental toughness to know that, when you are faced with a task, you complete it.

Forever Athletes take this approach to life and, inevitably, find success. By exhibiting these qualities, and by immersing yourself in your identity as a Forever Athlete, you can find success, too.

As a linebacker, there's something called "filling the gap," and it essentially means fitting into your defensive responsibility when the offense runs a play. Sounds simple, right? It's anything but that. Conceptually, this is an easy job. Go stand in between the guard and center, and make sure that the running back doesn't get by you. There's something you need to know, though.

The people across from you are going to do everything within their power to ensure that you don't succeed. Filling the gap isn't an easy task by any means. When you do this, you need to bring a relentless attitude and effort to have a shot at success. You need to have your fundamentals sound and your head on a swivel. There's no roundabout way of doing this in football.

If you want to be successful at this, you take it head-on, sometimes literally and figuratively. I've taken this same "fill the gap" concept and applied it to all things in life. When you are faced with a problem, you take it head-on.

You bring a relentless effort and conquer your problems. There's no dancing around the issue. You won't find success lying to yourself about the real problem at hand. You just need to strap on that helmet and meet that problem at the line of scrimmage. I can tell you firsthand that, if you don't, the problem will continue to come at you again and again.

As an athlete, you were able to learn things and put them to practice on a daily basis. You have been geared to find success under some of the most rigorous scenarios by putting in hard work, dedicating yourself to your craft, and doing things that others didn't have the heart to.

Never let a day go by that you don't use all of that to your advantage in your work, relationships, health, and overall life. The traits you possess as a Forever Athlete are rare and extremely valuable. Remember to keep that edge sharp, use your unique mindset to your benefit, and, when you need it the most, you will thrive.

ABOUT CODY

Cody Allen is a former collegiate athlete turned entrepreneur. He organizes informational and practicable fitness events and business development seminars, expressing both sides of his laudable career knowledge.

His years in the fitness space shine a light on how mental perspectives in competitive sports can improve a brand or company's exposure, performance, and success. As a result, he began outreach through Digital Cartel Media, teaching clients his approach to business with an athletic mindset pioneering the way.

His is a straightforward and practical formula in the digital world where content is king. Cody has developed a business strategy that comes directly from his days on the gridiron and focuses on discipline, innovation, and consistency. He has been featured on notable programming, including *Thrive Global, Yahoo! Finance, Business Insider, Medium*, and SportsGossip.com

Athletes live in a high-stress jungle. The margin between success and failure may be but a few seconds. The business world is similar, and Cody has found success by taking note of just that. Attacking each day with a relentless effort is exactly what Cody brings to the table in the business world and his life alike.

Remember Cody Allen's motto: "How you do anything is how you do EVERYTHING."

Connect with Cody:
Email: cody@thecodyallen.com
Socials: @thecodyallen

Chapter 13

THE ATHLETE'S SPIRIT
BY ERIKA FAY

The Jesuit scholar Hugo Rahner (cited in Lawrence, 2005) emphasizes the spiritual force of play and sport in his writings.

"To play," he explains, "is to yield oneself to a kind of magic ... to enter a world where different laws apply, to be relieved of all the weights that bear it down, to be free, kingly, unfettered and divine."

My guess is that if you are reading this book, it's because you are an athlete. I want to start by telling you how incredible I think you are and how much I admire you. Not just because you are an athlete, but the mere fact that you are investing time in reading this tells me that you are a growth-oriented person. You are invested in your life, your growth, and fulfilling your potential as a human being.

Just like you, I am an athlete. The level of competition and the sport I engage in has changed over the years, but I am an athlete. My journey to becoming an athlete was a bit nontraditional. As a child, I felt invincible, as most kids do! I knew I could do anything I put my mind to. After some years of realizing I wasn't great at everything I tried to do, I started to doubt myself and my skills.

Another thing that I was learning to live with was asthma. When I was a kid, it was severe. It wasn't the asthma attacks that created my self-doubt, even though they frequently put me in the hospital.

It was a voice in my head that told me I was incapable. I don't remember exactly how it progressed, but I do remember that one day in fifth grade, as we were all lining up, I felt like an outsider. I felt awkward, left out, and so uncomfortable in my body. Have you ever experienced a time when you felt completely out of place?

Feeling socially awkward and out of place rattled me. In retrospect, now that I have the awareness that our brains are wired for connection and that we have evolved to thrive as part of a community, the power of this experience and memory makes sense.

In his book, *Social,* renowned psychologist Matthew Lieberman discusses research in social neuroscience. He reveals that our need to connect with other people is even more fundamental, more basic, than our need for food or shelter. But, back then, the only conclusion I could come to was that there was something wrong with me.

I wasn't naturally gifted when it came to traditional sports like basketball, volleyball, tennis, or softball. Although I tried, it didn't feel right. I felt uncoordinated and had difficulty getting my body to do what I wanted it to do. Instead, the water was where I felt most comfortable.

As the quote above describes, I feel like I enter a different world when I swim; I feel free, not only physically, as the weight is literally lifted in the water but also on a soul level. I feel unfettered, playful, and, yes, even divine at times. I had some natural talent in swimming, and the pool is where I first learned how to harness my skill, focus, attention, energy, and body toward an athletic goal.

I found swimming during my sophomore year of high school, which is quite late. All the swimmers I knew had been with a swimming club since they were young. Regardless of this fact, I fell in love with all of it: being part of a team, the incredible feeling of being in the water, and my fantastic coach (shoutout to Jim Kesserling), who was able to see my potential and steer me into a stroke that I grew to love the backstroke.

Coach Jim taught me so many things and cultivated the determined, disciplined athlete I was becoming. I swam year-round once I discovered my passion for it, but I didn't set goals for myself as an athlete. I thought that I wasn't as good as the other kids, as that had been my experience with sports until then. During my senior year, with much coaching, direction, and challenge, I started to see that I could set goals and achieve them.

Coach Jim was the first person to work with me by means of visioning technology. He taught me to close my eyes and go through every second of the event in my mind, feel the feelings associated with the experience, and see the results I wanted to see.

This was a game-changer for me. I began to crush my time goals and became a strong contender for the number one spot in backstroke on a historically state championship-winning team, qualifying for State in my event. I caught the bug!

Once I realized I did have a natural talent that could be cultivated by focus and practice, I knew I wanted to continue in college. Enter water polo! As freshmen, a few other women and I started practicing with the men's water polo team. I suppose that no other women had ever practiced with the men before, and some of them clearly didn't want us there.

As a result, it didn't take us long to realize that we wanted our team, practice, tournaments, etc., and we started the first women's water polo team at Purdue University. I loved being a part of our team and having a space to challenge myself physically, mentally, and emotionally.

By then, I had been transformed from a kid who wasn't great at any sports and who never considered myself an athlete to a young woman who identified as an athlete. I remember at the end of my very last game as a senior, I laid on my back, floating in the water. I looked up at the ceiling of the natatorium, thinking to myself.

Okay, this is the end. Soak it in. Then I heard from another part of me, *What's next?* I know you can relate to that question.

To redirect my sadness about the end of water polo, I decided that my athletic endeavors would continue post-college. That's when I found endurance sports. It started with my mom running a marathon. I thought *if she can do it, then I can do it!*

I signed up for my first-ever marathon in 1996. It was the Madison Marathon in Wisconsin. The training and race itself were brutal experiences. I had no idea what I was doing and just went by my mom's old training schedule.

> " Once I realized I *did* have a natural talent that could be cultivated by focus and practice, I knew I wanted to continue in college. "

During the race, my mom met me at mile eighteen, and I remember her saying something like, "The next marathon will be better."

I snapped back, "There's not going to be a next marathon!"

When I finally crossed the finish line, around five and a half hours after I started, something changed for me. I started to think about the possibility of a next race. Perhaps it was that *what's next* voice in my head, or maybe it was because there was a part of me that really did enjoy testing the limits of my body and mind. About a week later, I decided that I'd try training for another marathon.

This time, I joined a running group and had a coach. The experience was still challenging, but it was way more fun! I met some girlfriends through the running community. I must specifically credit Lisa Zimmer, who is one of the owners of Fleet Feet Chicago.

Lisa had the genius idea to have Tuesday night "Chicks' Runs." I met some incredible women during this time who are still some of my closest friends to this day, and it's been over twenty years!

These women were up for trying out racing triathlons, and through this, I realized I loved the challenge of long distances. I started with a sprint distance triathlon and wound up doing numerous half Ironman

164

triathlons (1.2-mile swim, 56-mile bike, 13.1-mile run aka 70.3 miles total). I then moved on to two full Ironman distance triathlons (2.4-mile swim, 112-mile bike, 26.2-mile run, aka 140.6 miles total). The endurance journey is a whole other book, but at the time of this chapter being written, I have completed thirty-six full marathons and counting!

My goal is to complete a marathon in every US state and complete all six of the World Marathon Majors in Boston, Chicago, New York, Tokyo, London, and Berlin (I've done three of six as of right now!). I love the challenge, the community, and the opportunity to see new places around the world through running. I have had some of my most enjoyable experiences, as well as some of my lowest experiences, during endurance training and racing.

I feel like running, and endurance sports are two of the best ways to experience my life! And I have found something that I truly love. When I was younger and struggling to find a sport that I had any sort of skill at, if someone told me that I *would* find an athletic path that I loved, I wouldn't have believed them.

As a kid with severe asthma, I was close to death a few times. I am not being dramatic; I had several anaphylactic reactions that had me turning blue, and without an emergency room visit and, oftentimes, hospitalization, I would have died. I remember thinking as a kid: *Since I haven't died, there must be something powerful that I am meant to do with my life.*

I didn't know what that would look like, but I do remember thinking about it a lot as I was going through these episodes and surviving them.

Like many others, I was raised in a very spiritual household. My sister and I went to a Christian school for much of our childhood, attended church every Sunday, and our parents were involved in both a prayer group and a larger Chicago Catholic group.

Once I got to college, I began to challenge why I believed what I believed, what I thought about God and Spirit, and what this really had to do with my life. I think that love is a soul place. What does that mean? What if love is the very essence of Spirit? I've come to realize that, for me, Spirit, God, and love are synonymous.

For me, the path of athleticism began with discovering something I loved and felt adept at, which made me a part of something larger. I began to feel comfortable challenging myself. I've also used love as a method to guide my life and my career, which led me to become a marriage and family therapist, and, ultimately, a performance and transition coach for athletes.

As athletes, we usually gravitate to a particular sport because there is something about it that we love. Having an awareness of love is powerful. It can guide us on our unique path, whether it is in sport or outside of it. I invite you to pose some questions to yourself:

What *do* I love?
Whom do I love?
What *would* I love?

Although we can't see love physically (we can see expressions of kindness and acts of love), we know how real and powerful it can be. You have one unique life, and you are searching for ways to live more freely, so love and Spirit are at work in you. Your connection to Spirit is as unique as your thumbprint, and it speaks to you in the language of love through your longings, discontents, and what you would **love** for your life.

There is only one **you**. On this whole planet, only one of you exists. If you don't do you, you won't be done. Obviously, you are the only one in your body, and your body can and has done incredible things! But there's even more to you than that!

One of the ways athletes easily align with Spirit is through our sport. This has been evident to me throughout my journey, and by understanding the connection of Spirit/love and sport, perhaps you can see this in your life as well. See what you discover when you allow yourself to listen to the voice of love inside you.

Most of us have defined ourselves by what we do, and I did for a long time. I've come to learn that partnering with what I would love has opened my life in ways I would never have imagined and that I am way more than anything I do. I know you are more than anything you do as well. What if the practice of tuning in to love and living from that place is a direct representation of your uniqueness? And, what if, as you practiced living from love, you realized how incredible and how much more capable you are?

When you think about your athletic journey, do you remember feeling at home and aligned, which was reflected often in your athletic performance? I'd suggest that being *in the zone* while playing your sport comes from knowing you are exactly where you are meant to be and doing something you love. This doesn't mean that you never hear from your internal critic, which tries to make you doubt yourself and your abilities.

However, feeling that you are at home and doing what you are meant to do, you continue to raise the bar in any way you can through the drive to test your limits! You accept challenges, overcome obstacles, and then use them to get even better and to realize the next dream that previously felt completely out of reach. This is all accomplished with the knowledge that you are never done growing, getting better, or exceeding your best. This is because you are an athlete.

Look back at your athletic journey. Maybe it started with an awareness of possibilities and an ambition to achieve goals; this was when you became clear on your vision. It consisted of the results you wanted to create within your sport and in your life. You thought about not only what you deemed possible but also what you would love to do. Perhaps the vision evolved as you developed, and that's how it is supposed to work!

You see yourself there, in the vision. You can feel how it would feel to be the person living that life well before you get close to achieving it. You feel the pull to the image, you can see the dream realized and your goal fulfilled, and this gives you a sense of aliveness!

The feeling rises, and you think, *I'd love that!* You then commit to that dream, willing to do whatever it takes to get there. You begin to traverse the gap between where you are and where you would love to be.

Along the way, you move through resistance, challenges, limitations, and old beliefs that don't serve you. You do this by training, coaching, and keeping your focus on the vision of the dream fulfilled. Perhaps you are often faced with challenges or obstacles that make the vision seem out of reach, and the gap feels insurmountable.

You may, at times, feel separation from your dream or vision, but you keep your commitment to it and continue moving forward by focusing on seeing the fruits of your effort. You know growth is required, so you embrace it. You keep going. By means of this process, you become the person who achieves the vision.

You know how to do this in your life too, because you've been doing it as an athlete. I suggest that the challenge for all of us when we are done competing and seeking our next move (in our careers, relationships, or sports) is to start to experiment with living from a Spirit or Love place in all aspects of life. Looking back on how I gravitated toward swimming, water polo, and later to marathons, ironman triathlons, and even to my choice in careers, I notice a golden thread. It's love.

If we are engaged in a life we love, then we are living with the energy of fun and play that Hugo Rahner speaks of. What if growth and play are required for our spiritual evolution? Growth is always a spiritual journey to embody being "free, kingly, unfettered, and divine." What if your mission is to stay awake to the reality of who you really are—a spiritual being, love embodied—having a human experience?

You may hear from the voice of doubt, but you remind yourself that you are partnered with love and the Spirit of life itself. You recommit to clarity on what you love, and you go after it with fearless abandon.

What if life is one big spiritual journey, and the path we've traveled has led us to this perfect now? In every moment, we have the opportunity to choose aliveness as our compass as we continue to journey on in growth, in every aspect of life, even when our time competing has come to an end.

The voice of doubt inside me hasn't gone completely silent. But daily, I commit to partner with the Spirit in me, with love, to gain the courage I need to continue on my soul's path in sport and life, to serve who I am here to serve, and to become who I am here to become. I don't always do it perfectly, but I choose to endeavor to live from Spirit and love, and I invite you to live from the Spirit of love in you.

In closing, I'd love to share a quote by Dr. Michael Beckwith that can perhaps become a mantra as you close this book and head into your life:

"I am here to give birth to a greater and greater unfolding of my unique life."

Your athleticism is, was, and will always remain a part of you, whether you are still active in sport or not. As you continue to pay attention to what you would love, gain clarity on the kind of person you'd love to grow into (in an even greater way) and what you would love to contribute to this unique life, I'd argue that you are keeping your athlete's Spirit very much alive.

ABOUT ERIKA

Erika Fay, the founder of Maximum Achievement Coaching, is passionate about helping athletes create their ideal results on and off the field for even more freedom, fulfillment, and prosperity. Erika is a certified life mastery consultant and licensed psychotherapist, and success coach with over twenty years of experience working with professional and amateur athletes, entrepreneurs, and business professionals all around the world.

As a sought-after coach and international professional speaker, Erika specializes in delivering inspiring workshops, as well as transformational in-depth coaching programs with a dynamic approach that turns ideas into life-changing action to help clients achieve new heights of success.

She is a professional member of PAADS (Professional Association for Athlete Development Specialists), has contributed work to *Fete Lifestyle Magazine*, and has appeared on *Good Day Chicago*, the *Brian, Ali & Justin* morning radio show, and she has also been featured on the *Voice America* radio station.

Erika lives in Chicago with her partner and soon-to-be two-year-old son. As a former high school swimmer and water polo player at Purdue University, she has continued her own athletic pursuits as an endurance athlete. To date, she has completed two full Ironman-distance triathlons, thirty-five marathons (and counting!), and continues to compete in multiple marathons and triathlons per year.

Learn more about Erika and Maximum Achievement Coaching at www.maximumachievementcoaching.com.

Chapter 14

ATHLETE, THERAPIST, COMEBACK KID
BY SARAH FRITSCHE

In loving memory of Adeoluwa Olaniyan, a beautiful soul and talented athlete, called to God's Varsity team early.

The sun beamed on my skin and the buzzing of cicadas filled the air as I ran my fingers over the familiar texture of the basketball in my hands.

"Check!" I yelled from the end of the driveway, bouncing the ball to my younger brother, Matt, standing a few feet away.

"Let's go, Sarah!" he yelled back as he returned the ball to me. I began to dribble up the concrete toward the hoop when I heard another voice.

"Hey! Can I play?" Our neighbor, Zach, quickly approached and teamed up with my brother in a two-on-one pickup game. Not only was I already at a disadvantage, but then they had called dibs on playing as Michael Jordan and Scottie Pippen. I huffed and puffed as I bounced the ball back to the end of the driveway and called dibs on being John Stockton, a quality third choice but no "MJ."

As I drove to the basket, Zach punched the ball out of my reach and passed it to Matt, who easily scored.

This continued for three more plays before I stormed into the house, yelling, *"Why can't I ever be Jordan?"*

I found comfort in venting to my mother as she cooked dinner.

Her warm voice encouraged me to try again after decompressing, "Don't give up. Be proud of what you're doing out there," she said. After filling my lungs with a few deep breaths, I looked to the living room, where my father was watching the St. Louis Cardinals game.

"Sarah," he called out to me, "Just come watch the game with me for a while. McGuire is on deck!"

As seasons passed, I found myself immersed in an array of sports. A midwestern snowstorm just hit? No problem! My brother and I rounded up the other neighborhood kids for a pickup game of tackle football. Heavy rain? That meant perfecting our sliding techniques in the mud. Being one of the only girls on the field, I learned quickly to play aggressively and develop thick skin. Whenever my frustrations crept back, I remembered my mother's words and told myself to hang in there.

My family's privilege afforded my brother and me the ability to play organized sports ranging from tee-ball to karate. Our parents encouraged us to choose what we liked most and stick with it. While Matt initially chose soccer, basketball, football, and swimming, he ultimately followed my father's footsteps, focusing on baseball almost year-round. I followed a different path, starting out with swimming, gymnastics, soccer, figure skating, and horseback riding.

To this day, I am not sure how my parents managed our hectic schedules, on top of their own. Sports consumed our lives. But over the years, the abundance of activities began to feel overwhelming. I remember thinking, *I just want to be a kid, not go to practice every day.*

This feeling built up gradually, after many missed birthday parties and lazy evenings on the couch watching *Scooby Doo*. Sympathetic to the situation, my parents facilitated cutting back on some activities, helping me narrow my focus to running track and participating in competitive cheerleading.

These sports transitioned nicely from my kaleidoscopic athletic background. The power in my legs from figure skating and soccer aided in my sprinting abilities, and my history as a gymnast provided an optimal foundation for cheerleading.

This streamlined, middle school sports career began in sixth grade, with the addition of playing basketball. Seemingly foreshadowed by childhood pickup games, basketball was not my shining skill set. I was one of the tallest girls in my class, so I naturally played the center position. This was short-lived because when the other girls' height surpassed mine, I realized that the skills I'd acquired did not accommodate other positions that required better ball-handling skills and deeper range shooting.

Beginning in high school, I decided it was best to kick basketball to the curb. Throughout my track years, I ran various open sprints and relays, and I seemed to shock everyone during my shotput events, as my body type was generally shorter and slimmer than the other competitors. While I enjoyed track, I was not a fan of the constant shin splints and pulled muscles that came along with it. Man, that was so much running!

I quickly found myself feeling more passionate about cheerleading. As a freshman, I made the varsity competition team. I began independent tumbling lessons multiple times per week, in addition to daily practices.

During my senior year, my teammates unanimously voted me team captain, and I exploded with pride. I strived to be the best leader I could be. Riding the high, I became the first person at my tumbling gym to land one of the most difficult tumbling passes within the limits of our division. You could not tell me anything!

One night, I was perfecting my craft with my coach, Andrew. As I stretched and warmed up my tumbling passes, we joked about my trademark mismatching socks. It felt like a typical practice. I was in my zone and everything was flowing. I positioned myself at the edge of the blue mat, looked at Andrew on the opposite end, and began my signature bunny hop lead-in to four running steps.

I jumped forward, propelled by my alternating hands and feet bouncing off the mat. I felt powerful and graceful, as if my body was a well-oiled, gymnastic automaton, built to tumble over the ground and float through the air. The second time my feet returned to the mat was to push my body from a roundoff back handspring into a back-tuck.

Essentially, this is a high-flying backflip with no hands. I was moving swiftly but soon realized that something had gone awry. I did not gather my usual power, as I transitioned into the back-tuck. It was low to the ground and felt sloppy.

After I landed on both feet, I heard Andrew yelling, "Oh my God! Are you okay?"

I looked over at him, initially confused. I knew I had not thrown a great tumbling pass, but I did not think it was *that* bad. Not even ten seconds later, my heart sank into my stomach as I felt a sharp pain in the side of my foot. I collapsed onto the mat as the coaches ran to my aid.

Andrew explained, "You jumped off a rolled ankle! Your right ankle was literally sideways! How did you even land that?" I was not sure if I should laugh or cry, and what came out was a weird combination of both.

Andrew, who was of similar stature to me at the time, carried me out of the gym and drove me home. Of course, this specific evening, my brother's legion baseball team was playing in a double-header playoff game. So, I was on my own until my family returned home. I tried napping on the couch while I waited, but the pain was excruciating.

So, I hopped on one leg to the kitchen to find a bottle of ibuprofen. About an hour later, my parents and brother returned home, two wins happier. I held back tears as I explained what had happened. My mother, a nurse, drove me to her hospital for evaluation.

"Well, it looks like you broke your fourth and fifth metatarsals and have a high ankle sprain," the emergency room doctor said, pointing at my X-ray. "We will put you in a boot until you heal up." His voice slowly faded as I sunk into myself and started crying uncontrollably.

I was in shock. How did I hurt myself throwing a tumbling pass I threw every single day? It could have at least been while I was doing something cooler! Either way, I was sidelined for nearly all of first semester, missing football games and several competitions. Completely beside myself, I wondered how I could be a worthy captain from the sidelines.

Nobody tells you what it is like to suddenly lose such a big part of your life. My daily routine was completely disrupted. Not only was I unable to participate for months, but I was also pulled away from my teammates to attend physical therapy. My support system was ripped away when I needed it most.

Worst of all, my body had betrayed me. Everyday tasks were difficult to manage, and I relied on family and friends to help me with actions that I previously took for granted. My arms ached over the padding of my crutches, and my hands became raw from gripping the handles.

My foot constantly throbbed. But my experience of physical pain was far surpassed by my mental distress. I watched my muscle definition wear away, I lost my appetite, and I felt an overbearing sadness. I was utterly unmotivated and preferred to stay in bed whenever I could.

I told myself that I only had two options at that point: give up sports completely and let the injury win or fight for my passion and regain my sense of self. From that moment, the injury lit a fire under me. I knew my body would heal, but I had to bring my mind on board. I dedicated as much time as I safely could to physical rehabilitation and mental preparation.

My hard work paid off, as I was back in action during the second semester for basketball season and state-wide competitions. I finally felt like myself again, especially showing off my new tumbling pass on the basketball court to what felt like the entire school. This was also when people started to notice that I was the team captain, which further bolstered my pride and cemented my identity.

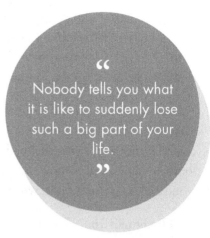

" Nobody tells you what it is like to suddenly lose such a big part of your life. "

After a successful end to senior year, there was no question in my mind that I wanted to continue competing at a high level. Once I visited Lindenwood University and realized that their cheerleading program is one of the best in the country, I knew it was the perfect fit. I brought my A-game to tryouts and felt elated when I made the team. A week after packing my bags and moving in, cheer camp began: nine hours of strenuous practice daily for five consecutive days.

Camp was juxtaposed with summer break: our recovery time, filled with whatever we wanted for two months with no consequences. Camp was always a wake-up call to whip ourselves back into shape, as evidenced by our bodies, so sore that we could barely bend our legs to sit down. Luckily, the only people on campus to witness this were other athletes who understood our struggles.

Shortly after camp commenced, I realized just how talented the other cheerleaders were. I was no longer a big fish in a small pond. We were all big fish, and the pond was more like a lake. I would be lying if I said that this did not shake my confidence a bit. However, it motivated me to work even harder to prove that I deserved a spot on the team.

While I experienced several highs and lows during my freshman season, I did not lose my passion or sense of identity within the sport. I realized that my role would look different than what I was accustomed to, so I humbled myself and kept my nose to the ground. I quickly learned that along with the sport itself, my schedule was also more demanding at this level.

I formed new routines and habits and even chose my outfits based on practice time. Being an athlete on campus was like a badge of honor, and I reveled in the recognition from my peers, especially when sporting team gear.

I will never forget the excitement I felt the first time I stepped foot on the dew-coated turf for the home-opening football game. The band blared the fight song as I nervously tried to remember each motion of our routine. I could not take my eyes off the crowd as I smiled, hoping that nobody could sense it was my first time out there. My eyes dashed over to a familiar couple in the stands, clapping their hands joyously.

Realizing it was my parents who had come to support me during this milestone in my life, I felt loved and embraced in my new role. Once the game ended, I was met with a rush of empowerment. I had cheered in my first-ever college game, and I'd done it in front of family and friends! I could have lived in that moment for an eternity.

My parents soon met me at the exit of the stadium and exclaimed, "We're taking you out to eat! Wherever you want to go!"

At that moment, I could have easily walked to my dorm and changed into something more comfortable. However, I wanted to keep my sparkly black and gold uniform on and that obnoxious bow in my hair for as long as I possibly could, showing them off to everyone in town.

While this glitter-filled euphoria lasted throughout the football and basketball seasons, I knew that our competition season was quickly approaching. In college cheerleading, one of the biggest national competitions takes place in Daytona Beach, Florida, in the spring. At Lindenwood, a spot on the gameday performance squad did not guarantee a spot on the nationals' roster. In the winter, coaches held a separate, and rather grueling, tryout for those interested in competing.

After implementing additional workouts and finding every possible open gym in town to perfect my tumbling passes, I felt prepared for tryouts. Despite my confidence in my performance, waiting for the roster to be posted was torturous. I felt constantly on edge, checking my email incessantly. Finally, my name jumped off the screen at me, and I screamed in joy. I called my parents immediately to share the good news. What an honor! I wanted to tell the world!

After months of hard work, injuries, arguments, and exhaustion, the long-anticipated day had arrived. There I was, nineteen years old, competing on a national platform in front of the beach and a huge audience!

What I had previously known as nerves did not compare to what I felt as my teammates and I walked backstage to prepare for our routine. My body was shaking. My skin formed goosebumps, despite the scorching heat. Lil Wayne's *Dedication 2* mixtape was blaring in my headphones until the moment our team was called to the bandshell. I approached my starting spot on the royal blue mat, and the rest was a blur.

Adrenaline took over my body, calling upon pure muscle memory to complete the routine.

After what felt like the blink of an eye, I was running off the mat with my teammates. Sensing the overall energy, I knew that we had not executed our routine to our fullest potential. The silence was deafening, and anxiety was written all over our faces. As we exited the bandshell, I heard my teammates arguing about what went wrong. The disappointment sunk in when we huddled to listen to our coaches' final feedback.

While a range of emotions surged through my body as I stood, arms interlocked with my teammates, embarrassment was not one of them. The camaraderie was a blessing, and I was reminded of that many times throughout my career. I would go to war with them!

Fast forward to my sophomore year. I once again earned a spot on the nationals' team. Two consecutive years was quite an accomplishment! Falling so low in the rankings the previous year had lit a fire under our asses, and we approached competition season with a vengeance. One evening, we began learning the pyramid for a section of our routine. As a base of the three-tier pyramid structure, my role was to hold a woman who was holding another woman.

I stood confidently at the bottom layer, strategically placing my hands and feet for optimal balance. The weight of the bodies above me was heavy, but I was strong.

This is what I've been working out so hard for, I told myself. Our first two attempts at the pyramid crumbled, which was relatively common while learning new stunts. Our third attempt started remarkably smoothly, as we nailed the opening sequence. I heard our coaches clapping and yelling for us, followed by the flash of arms and legs crashing down toward me.

As I caught my falling teammates, I felt a sharp pain in my knee. I fell to the mat and instantly began sobbing.

"Your knee popped so loud!" one teammate yelled in horror.

In the scramble of the fall, one of my teammates stepped sideways on my bent knee, creating an inverted V-shape.

Not this again, I thought to myself, as that familiar feeling rushed back. After being escorted to the athletic trainer's office, I experienced an unusual sensation, which I compared to a ball of rubber bands inside my knee. In shock, I called my parents, who wanted me to see a specialist at the hospital where my mother worked. The only problem was his limited availability. I booked the first available appointment for X-rays and MRIs, which was a month after the injury itself.

Waiting was the worst part because I held out hope to return for the season. My coaches did not think my injury was serious, and the trainers initially told me they felt no evidence of a torn anterior cruciate ligament (ACL).

Because I could walk without crutches, we all felt optimistic. A few weeks after my appointment, I received results from the specialist, revealing that I had completely torn my ACL and meniscus, in addition to fracturing my tibia. I later learned that loose ACLs are common among past gymnasts, so the trainers could not differentiate between my torn right ligament and intact left one.

Once again, I was sidelined for the remainder of the season, undergoing reconstructive surgery. This was the first time I significantly lost sight of my athletic identity, falling into a depression and questioning whether I wanted to rejoin the team.

Rehabilitation was a slow process that removed me from practices, workouts, and worst of all, nationals. I felt disconnected from my peers and lost my confidence. My body felt foreign, with the sudden change in activity and functionality.

While I thought I was more prepared after having one major injury under my belt, this one hit me even harder. I was forced to look at myself as someone other than an athlete. Halfway through my college career, I did not expect to be faced with the devastating possibility that I may not return to sports.

Who was I, if not an athlete? My other identities emerged: student, daughter, friend, woman, sister, creator. While I tried to embrace these other facets of myself, they simply did not compare to the rush of being an athlete. I felt alone, almost spiteful toward my peers who had never sustained an injury. Did anyone understand what I was going through?

With these thoughts spiraling in my mind, I decided to return to cheerleading my junior year and try out for the national team a third time.

Tryouts fell at the cusp of my clearance to return to full activity, so I was cautioned not to go overboard. However, something took over me once I stepped back onto the practice mat. I remembered the overwhelming sadness I'd felt for months after my injury. This was my time to reclaim my identity.

The passion I had almost forgotten about came rushing to the forefront. My spark was back! I knew that I must pull out all the stops to make the nationals team again. With the coaches' help, I put my best foot forward and successfully made the team.

Tears of joy streamed down my face when I received the news. I worked my ass off to return to pre-injury form, both physically and mentally. Let me tell you, it was one of the hardest things I had done to that point! I was plagued by chronic pain, mistrust of my body, wavering confidence, and mental blocks, but striving toward redemption of the national title kept me motivated.

Well, it seemed the universe had other plans for me. Two weeks before our bus was scheduled to leave for Florida, I woke up to a sharp pain in my right side. Sweat rolled down my skin as my body temperature skyrocketed. I alternated vomiting and applying a heating pad to my side until it exploded in the microwave.

Dismissing this as the stomach flu, I figured I could sleep it off. After ten hours of pain, I finally asked my parents to drive me to the emergency room, where I was met with unfortunate news. My appendix was moments away from rupturing, and doctors immediately prepped me for surgery. Once again, I was sidelined for nationals. At this point, I felt as if I was cursed. Maybe this was just not meant to be.

I was mentally and physically exhausted. Did I really want to keep sacrificing my body and time to attend practice every day? No, I wanted to sleep in. I wanted to hang out with friends after class. I wanted to enjoy my last year of college with little stress.

So, after much contemplation and exploration of my priorities, I decided to hang my uniform in the rafters for my senior year. This was one of the hardest choices I made as an athlete, especially after such an anti-climactic end to my career. While part of me felt unsatisfied and unfulfilled, especially without the constant grind, another part of me felt free for one of the first times in my life.

I no longer had to worry about injuries, being late to practice, getting yelled at by coaches, finding time to eat, or staying up late to finish homework. But, of course, there were tradeoffs. I no longer had a built-in support system of peers who experienced similar joys and struggles. I no longer was forced to stay active. I no longer received special recognition or status on campus. I no longer had something to satisfy my competitive nature.

Most of all, I no longer could call myself a current athlete. I adopted the mindset and identity of a "former athlete." This seemed to imply that I was somehow shutting that piece of myself down forever. It was heartbreaking, as up until that point, I had lived, breathed, and bathed sports. My name had been synonymous with competitive cheerleading for over ten years. What was I supposed to do? Where was the handbook for life after sports?

While I used much of my newfound free time to enjoy some typical activities of a college senior, such as traveling for spring break, going to parties and bars with friends, and gathering for hours in the common areas on campus, I missed the sense of pride and belonging that sports provided.

The need to explore other aspects of my identity was once again pervasive, but I had no idea where to start. I knew those parts of me existed, but they did not inspire me. At times, I felt lost, and I wished someone could guide me through the transition.

I wondered if my family felt the same sense of pride when they thought of me as a student, rather than a student-athlete. I wondered if peers viewed me as a quitter because I did not stick to my sport for one more year. I wondered if I had let the team down.

Did I make the right choice, or had I let myself down, too? All the *what if*'s constantly ran through my mind. Reminiscing about my time as a cheerleader, I played back my reels of highlights, bloopers, and disappointments on the movie screen in my brain. Did I give up too soon?

To make things even more confusing, the team that competed at nationals that year won first place. Damn it; one more year and I could have earned a ring! My thoughts quickly spiraled into processing my life story as an athlete. I pondered my unique experiences and the intertwined role sports had on the fabric of my family structure.

Would my family dynamics change? Would I even want to watch sports now that I had retired, or would it be too painful? Would it bring up thoughts of what could have been? How would I introduce myself to new people without telling them that I am an athlete? In my mind, I was doomed to being boring, old Sarah. How could people relate to me now? I had lost my edge!

Now, I know what you are thinking. *Sarah, cut the dramatics!* But this was the reality I was living in. I could not fathom my future without sports. Soon, something inside me flipped like a light switch, and I thought, *Maybe I can change my relationship with athletics.*

While I would no longer compete at the collegiate level, I might be able to integrate sports into my life in novel ways. This thought was a diamond in the rough, proving to be a life-changing blessing.

As I finished my senior coursework and began researching graduate programs I stumbled upon a psychological specialization area called sport psychology.

No way, I thought, *this must be a sign!* I had a passion for psychology, but combining the two? This was the best thing since sliced bread! I found a dual counseling and sport psychology program at the University of Missouri and fell head over heels for the idea. After graduating from Lindenwood, I was accepted into the program and once again packed my bags.

I immediately felt at home, as my classes were filled with students and professors who were former athletes, each with their own unique stories. Many of my assignments focused on real world sports scenarios and controversies from a psychological lens. I knew I found my calling. This seemed to be the closest substitution for my experiences as a college athlete.

The transition was seamless, and my cohort became a close-knit group, navigating the challenges of graduate school together with grace and humor. While I felt this sense of community, something was still missing. I longed to experience being part of a team and competing at a high level. While I could not participate in organized sports at the graduate level, I learned that Mizzou offered a refreshing number of intramural sports.

Shortly after this discovery, I recruited a group of friends to join a sand volleyball team. Despite never playing organized volleyball, I was excited about the challenge. My team played for two seasons and finished with a .500 record.

We were far from the best team out there, but damn, did we have fun! Although it was not the high-level competitive experience that I was craving, I could finally call myself the coveted title of athlete once again.

My experiences at the University of Missouri propelled me into further studies at The Chicago School of Professional Psychology, where I am currently pursuing my Doctorate of Clinical Psychology.

Moving to Chicago was yet another change of scenery for me, but it proved to be a fruitful one. From day one, I have focused much of my coursework, clinical work, and research within the realm of sport psychology. I am even writing my dissertation on the psychological effects of injury on female college athletes. Coincidence? Of course not.

People often ask me what exactly sport psychology is. I am ecstatic that it is a growing field, which utilizes psychological knowledge and skills to address sport-related issues. Areas of intervention can include performance enhancement, developmental and social aspects of sports, systemic issues within sport settings, and the overall wellbeing of athletes. This is commonly combined with clinical aspects of psychology, such as addressing depression, anxiety, and post-traumatic stress disorder.

The field has gained traction with the movement of many high-level athletes openly discussing mental health. Advocates include Kevin Love, Brandon Marshall, Michael Phelps, Usain Bolt, Simone Biles, and Naomi Osaka, to name a few.

Some studies estimate that around 35%-40% of high-level athletes experience mental health concerns that manifest in crisis situations and burnout. One goal of sport psychology is to prevent this from happening by addressing the root of the issues and managing symptoms.

The opportunity to provide these services to multi-level athletes across various settings has solidified my passion. I become invested in their stories and their seasons, exploring challenges they face along the way, and sharing my wisdom. My clients teach me just as much as I teach them. They are truly inspiring!

I have also been blessed to connect with mentors in the field who have guided me through the seemingly never-ending process of schooling, licensure, and certification. My professors have fostered my interests and understood me through the lens of both a student and an athlete. These experiences have all helped me reconnect with parts of myself that could have easily dissipated after college cheerleading.

In many ways, my athletic identity has informed my work. My background in competitive sports helps me break the trust barrier and build relationships with athletes I work with. This is especially important as a young woman in a male-dominated vocation. My clients often express relief when they learn that I was an athlete, and that they do not have to explain the system to me. Therapy sessions flow much more fluently with this understanding.

The values, lessons, and dedication I derived from sports help me to be an effective therapist. Similar to my experiences in organized sports, graduate school and therapy work have structured systems in place. There are parallels between the roles of coaches and supervisors, professors and teammates, classmates and coworkers, and mentors and mentees.

All parts must work together like a well-oiled machine in order to produce the desired results. Trust, communication, and discipline are at the forefront.

Through the years, I have come to learn that life is about perspective. When the relationship with one facet of your life changes, that does not mean it is over. This is how I reconciled my doubts about retiring from cheerleading. I changed my perspective to uncover new ways of interacting with sports. Easier said than done, right? When I work with athletes today, I constantly hear concerns and struggles that mirror my experiences.

If you have played sports at a high level, or even at all, you can likely pinpoint several examples of this identity crisis phenomenon for yourself. What is it about an athletic identity that makes it so powerful, exclusive, and prideful?

Is it the collaboration of diverse peers who may not otherwise come together? Is it the adrenaline you feel when stepping foot on the field? Is it the recognition from society? Is it the constant grind that gives you a sense of purpose? I encourage you to ponder this. Think about what sports mean to you. Think about the role they have played in your life.

As a therapist, I encourage my clients to think about their identities in a multifaceted way, so as not to be faced with confusion when one aspect is pushed to the backseat. Research shows that when we possess multiple strong identities, rather than one, increased states of confidence and overall wellbeing occur.

Thus, negative emotions may be experienced less severely when we feel a sense of loss within one of these identities. Without my rollercoaster of an experience in college cheerleading, I may not be able to provide therapeutic insight in this area.

With time, I have realized that there is no such thing as a "former" athlete. Even when I am no longer able to play sports, I will forever be an athlete. So, cheers to those reading this who know exactly what I am talking about. Continue to embrace that inner fire, even if that means channeling it in new ways.

You, too, are a Forever Athlete!

Well, my friends, if you have not learned anything else from this chapter, you know one thing for certain: I will always find my way back to sports. You have my family to thank for raising me in a sport-enmeshed environment, where playing and watching sports were unspoken traditions.

You have my brother to thank for lighting my competitive fire by always challenging me, even when the game was unfair. My parents can take credit for raising me to believe that I can play any sport I desire, fostering resilience and confidence that I carry with me to this day.

If you walked into my parents' house, you would almost certainly find Matt, his best friend Doug, and my parents discussing whatever game is on TV and how their fantasy teams are doing. When I visit, I can count on holding at least one mock fantasy draft over dinner.

Without these experiences, my life path would have likely looked completely different. I may not have ended up in the field of psychology, much less sport psychology. I am so grateful to have such a supportive, non-judgmental, and loving family that constantly makes me feel like I can conquer any challenge presented to me.

The next generation is off to a great start with my nephew, who already cannot get his fill of watching and playing every sport he can dream of.

Oh, and one more thing.

You did not think I would end my athletic journey there, did you? My life in Chicago would not be complete without my newfound love for flag football. Shortly after moving, I decided to pursue a dream I'd had since the days I spent with the neighborhood kids. For now, football feeds the competitive beast inside me, so I plan on playing until my body tells me that I must once again hang up my jersey.

Although I have experienced my fair share of injuries, I do not foresee retiring in the near future. So, if you find yourself interested in watching some flag football games in the middle of January, come stop by and say hello in Florida for our national tournament. It is funny how life comes full-circle sometimes.

What can I say? I guess it really was meant to be after all!

I'm coming for that ring!

ABOUT SARAH

Sarah Fritsche is a doctoral student in clinical psychology at The Chicago School of Professional Psychology in Chicago, Illinois. She earned her Master of Counseling and Sport Psychology from the University of Missouri in Columbia, Missouri, and her Bachelor of Psychology from Lindenwood University in St. Charles, Missouri.

After graduation in 2023, Sarah will pursue a career as a licensed clinical and sport psychologist within a university setting. She has provided therapeutic services to adolescents, college students, multi-performance level athletes, and older adults across settings such as university athletic departments and counseling centers, middle schools, inpatient substance use treatment centers, and neuropsychological clinics.

Sarah has also created and facilitated multiple mindfulness and meditation groups within university settings in addition to her involvement in programs like Girls in the Game, the Social Justice Leadership Academy, the Hip-Hop Heals Community of Practice, and the Expressive Arts Association.

She has contributed to the field of research in sport psychology and mental health through publications and presentations at multiple conferences and forums. Sarah's work is informed by her experience as a collegiate student-athlete, as well as her interests in social justice, mindfulness practice, trauma-informed theory, and community mental health.

Connect with Sarah:
Instagram: @Therapist_Bae3
Email: sfritsche@ego.thechicagoschool.edu

Chapter 15

A WAKE-UP CALL TO GREATNESS

BY GAVIN MCHALE

I t started off the same way many hockey fights do.

Two players were battling just outside my crease, directly in front of my face as I tried to locate the puck. I hacked the opposition across the back of his legs while the Portland Winterhawks powerplay snapped the puck around, awaiting their best opportunity to really bury us.

My defensemen and their fighter jostled for position and wielded their sticks like two-by-fours, a sign I should've noticed before everything went down. Finally, one of them took it further than the other felt was fair. The gloves flew off and I heard the combatants swearing at each other as the first punches were thrown and all 10,000 fans in Portland's Rose Garden began to roar.

This was what they came for.

I was no stranger to the rough and tumble Western Hockey League in 2005, just a few years removed from bench-clearing brawls and fights so bad they had to have teams warm up separately to avoid confrontation. This New Year's Eve battle was going to provide everything the crowd wanted for their twenty-dollar ticket. The Hawks and the Thunderbirds from up the highway in Seattle were going at it.

Immediately, another fight broke out to my right, then another up near the blue line, and before I knew it, the rest of the players had joined the pile in front of me. They were chucking knuckles as the referee pulled out his notepad to take numbers and called the linesmen off. When shit like this went down, they let us tire each other out—no need to get themselves hurt with an errant fist.

But I was a goalie, and even though I was in the midst of it, I wasn't supposed to fight. That wasn't in the playbook. It was only during the craziest of fights, maybe once a year, that goalies dropped the mitts.

I had never been the type to fight. In fact, I was so nonconfrontational that my coaches had to put me in goal when I was eight years old. I wouldn't even try to fight for a loose puck. It wasn't in my DNA.

But on this night, after the shit I'd gone through leading up to this, I said, "Fuck it." Although this moment was not significant to me at the time, other than the painful broken nose I earned, I see it now as an inflection point that taught me one of the greatest lessons I'd ever learn in my life, one that I struggle to this day to follow.

Only a few weeks before that night, I had turned 18 years old. Like most kids that age, I thought I knew everything there was to know about the world.

It was my NHL draft year and was certainly not going as planned. I had a girlfriend back home whom I had fallen hard for, and all I wanted to do was spend time talking to her. I was sick of the pressure of hockey, and she provided a release, an escape hatch into a different world.

I could be a normal high school graduate with her. I could be a kid with her.

She liked me and accepted me for who I was, and a part of me really needed that at the time.

My mind was in a different place, and my play had slid dramatically. As you do when you're eighteen years old and your massive ego is challenged, I started to blame everyone else. My teammates were missing defensive assignments, they weren't very good, or they didn't play well in front of me on that particular night. My coaches weren't giving me the opportunity I thought I deserved. Hockey was keeping me from my girlfriend, and it wasn't fair.

Little did I know, I was authoring my own fate ... and I was writing it in ink.

One day in November, near the end of a particularly bad stretch of games and an equally shitty week of practice, our assistant coach pulled me aside as we left the ice. Most junior teams have three different assistant coaches, and you can bet that there will always be a young one full of piss and vinegar; ours was a dickhead.

Then there's the goalie coach, usually an oddball who kept to himself, and ours fit the bill. Finally, there was the sage, the wise and slightly older father figure who often mentored the head coach. This was the guy who pulled me aside.

As we were standing in our makeshift workout room inside the practice rink (which was an old, converted grocery store—I'm not even kidding), he laid down the truth for me.

"Have you ever heard of a self-fulfilling prophecy, Gav?"

"No," I said while thinking, *What the fuck is that?*

"Well, you're not getting the playing time you want, so you've decided to be angry about that and slack off in practice. I can see it happening a lot lately. You're blaming your teammates, and you're being a bad teammate yourself. And yet, you expect that to make us give you more playing time, but instead, it's just making it easier for us *not* to play you. Does that make sense?"

The truth is it made total sense. I hated every single syllable that came out of his mouth, but it made so much sense that it hurt. My frustrated ego screamed in my head.

"Yeah, it does," I responded solemnly.

As you'd expect, with no tools or skills to deal with failure, and zero experience with anything but being the absolute best while pretending to be humble, I went right back to the very same behavior that got me into that mess.

This horror story continued to be written, despite everyone else's best efforts to create a happy ending. About a week later, our starting goalie, the best goalie in the league at the time, hurt his ankle and I became *the guy*.

Although his injury benefitted me, it hurt almost everyone else around me. But I couldn't see that. I was numb to anyone's needs but my own. I remember celebrating in front of him when he told me the news. What an asshole I must've looked like, dancing around the locker room. This guy had just found out his MVP season was in jeopardy, along with our team's chances at a playoff spot, and here I was celebrating.

I'd finally got the chance I felt I deserved. This was my chance to show my coaches they were wrong, to show the NHL scouts they should pick me, to show my girlfriend I was a superstar in the making, and to prove to my parents that all the time and money invested in me was worth it.

But none of that happened.

In the days leading up to that fateful New Year's Eve game in Portland, things became much worse. I couldn't win a game after Christmas break to save my life (or before Christmas, for that matter), and my attitude and commitment to the team had become secondary to my commitment to the narrative that I was a bad boy, I no longer gave a shit and I was untouchable.

My coaches, the very ones who had warned me weeks earlier, chose to play a fifteen-year-old call-up goalie ahead of me in the New Year's Eve game in what I felt was the ultimate *fuck you* to a player who had been grinding it out all season waiting for his chance.

I was furious. I pouted on the bus for the entire three-hour drive to Oregon. I barely put in any effort in warm-ups, making it clear to anyone watching and to my teammates that I would not be the starting goalie that night. I scowled in the locker room as my teammates prepared to play a huge game in front of tons of fans. These were the games junior hockey players lived for.

I sulked at the end of the bench, watching the first one and a half periods of the game, hoping the call-up goalie would get shelled. I even grumbled as the coach tapped me on the shoulder to replace him after Portland scored their fifth goal and the game was getting out of hand.

I had stopped giving any shits what anyone thought of me. I now know this is a good thing, but my intentions at that moment were way off base. Inside my helmet, a war was taking place between the up-and-coming draft prospect and my dickhead of an ego, kicking and screaming for attention.

So, here we were. Standing in the crease at the Rose Garden in Portland, looking up at a lopsided scoreboard and 10,000 fans just waiting for me to get bulldozed. I had never felt lonelier in my life, especially since deep down I knew I was the one who had pushed all my teammates, the soldiers I was in the trenches with, as far away as possible to protect myself.

The game had turned into a tire fire. It was time to give the American hockey fans the bare-fisted brawl they were looking for, and boy did I ever do that. As I saw the fights unfolding around me, I did the opposite of what my normal instincts would be. Wires crossed. Everything was already going wrong in every way.

So, I thought, *how much worse could it be?*

Careful to keep my gloves and helmet on so none of the goons could hit me, I used my stick in an attempt to direct traffic, trying to hook my blade around one of their players' bodies. It must have looked like a spear from the other end of the ice. When things got a little too heated in one pile, I skated to another pile of fighters, pretending to know what I was doing with my back to their goalie, who was barreling down the ice at full speed, shedding his stick and gloves.

Before I knew it, he had turned me around, flipped my helmet over the back of my head, and we were squared off.

Fuck it.

I dropped my gloves, grabbed his jersey, and took a big swing that missed by a mile, completely exposing myself as I lurched forward. Then it hit me. The other goalie's fist obliterating my nose was the culmination of that terrible season. It was a microcosm of the shitshow that had been my life for the previous six months, a shitshow that I had authored, just like this fight.

My nose popped, spraying blood everywhere, and my eyes went blurry with tears. I took a few more punches to the side of my head until I crumpled, and I distinctly remember the clean, white stripe on the arm of my jersey turning crimson as my left arm braced my fall to the ice.

Then it all went dark. This fight, this moment in front of 10,000 screaming Oregonians loving every second of a group of teenagers beating the shit out of one another, taught me absolutely nothing at the moment or the days following.

I called my parents from the bus as they were enjoying the New Year's Eve celebrations back home and my voice, altered by the two plugs up my nose, gave me away in a second. When we arrived in Seattle in the wee hours of January 1st, 2006, I enjoyed the pleasure of having a steel rod shoved up my left nostril and cranked to rebreak my nose back into its rightful place.

I was traded ten days later, in the first event that would start the dominoes quickly falling on the end of my chances at a career in professional hockey. More disagreements with coaches, losses, blaming of teammates, and trades sealed the deal. But as I look back on these events fifteen years later, I'm reminded that I was the author of my own fate that night, and for the entire season that led up to it. I also know that I have been the author of my own fate every single second since then.

If you take anything from this story, other than the best way to lose a hockey fight, take this:

When it comes to the good times, know that you created those by putting your head down and doing the work required. By willingly accepting failure as your friend, you can create an incredible reality for yourself.

Regarding the bad times, we both know that you allowed these into your life in some way or another. Or, in the case of events completely outside your control like sickness or death of people close to you, your response is always within your control.

Once competitive hockey officially ended for me, five years after that fateful fight in Portland, I graduated university with a degree in Kinesiology. After a few experiences I'd rather forget as an employee, I decided to venture out on my own in the business world.

I came up fast in the fitness industry, building myself a nice little personal training business in my first couple of years. I was busy. I was making good money by societal standards. However, a pattern was emerging; I had chosen something I was already good at, then followed society's rules to win, taking the shortest and easiest possible route to get there.

Still, I was absolutely exhausted, and I knew there was no way I could live the lifestyle I wanted or have a family if I kept going at that pace. It was not sustainable. I was working too much for the money I was earning, and I knew there had to be a better way.

So, I struck out to find one, and I came across a new industry which was just emerging. Online training was the new frontier, and I knew that's what I needed—a way to earn a little more money, something that would allow me to help a few more people and work a little less.

No matter how hard I tried, no matter how badly I consciously wanted something different from my current situation—just like I had in hockey, nothing was moving the needle. I could have written a textbook on the business strategies I learned over the next two years. But I could not, for the life of me, make them work for me. After investing over $20,000 and seeing almost no return, I got frustrated. I became jaded. I started blaming everyone else, even social media algorithms, for my lack of success in comparison to the success others were having. Sound familiar?

This continued until I met a coach who made it all make sense for me. His name was Zander, and he shared with me the same lesson a fist to the face had tried and failed to teach me a decade and a half earlier:

You create or allow everything in your life.

Still, I struggled to put it into practice, like the promising young goalie who couldn't get his shit together. When faced with uncomfortable situations to help me grow, I retreated into old patterns. I chose comfort and stayed right where I was.

However, there was one subtle change. I became aware of these actions, and the consequences they brought, no longer making blind decisions that didn't serve me. After months of challenge, I prevailed.

Having gone through the negative experience I did with hockey, I only knew what I *didn't* want to feel again; I didn't want to feel like I had left something in the tank. I couldn't face the reality again that I had orchestrated my own demise. I began taking responsibility and making decisions from a place of purpose, no matter how difficult they were. I took action and looked fear directly in the face, smirking at it.

I now know, without a shadow of a doubt, that this was the missing piece of the puzzle that had led to my defeat in the hockey world. Could I have made it? Maybe. I probably had the skill. But hindsight is always twenty/twenty. If I knew then what I know now, I would've taken responsibility for my situation. I would have put my head down and dove headfirst into the tough stuff, no matter how much my ego kicked, screamed, and told me to stop.

At that point, another lesson I'd learned from hockey came to the forefront: you cannot change the past. The goal that slipped past me and already went in … *went in.* But I could always change the future. I could always stop the next puck. I began to welcome failure and take an objective view of my daily habits and mistakes. I embraced the messiness that comes with learning and growing and allowed myself to finally enjoy the process.

My business grew, along with my bank account. I was helping more people and making more money without running myself ragged, all because I decided to take responsibility and make a change. I have since shifted from training clients to coaching other trainers, and the challenges keep showing up. Now, I'm ready to learn the lessons.

If you want to attack the game we call life like the athlete you are, then it's time to step up and take responsibility for your central role in it. You can let losses and challenges take you down the path of resentment, which comes with a long, slow return to respect. Or you can let failure teach you and help you grow, knowing that struggle is not only expected but required to become the person you want to be.

> "
> I embraced the messiness that comes with learning and growing and allowed myself to finally enjoy the process.
> "

I've finally learned (or at least allowed myself to accept) that I am always in control of my own fate, and it's the hard times that allow us to grow … but only if we let them.

ABOUT GAVIN

Gavin McHale was on the fast track to playing professional hockey when he ran into the most common roadblock an athlete can face: his own limiting beliefs.

Now that he's been able to face his fears and build two flourishing businesses post-hockey, he's on a mission to connect others to their highest potential, using failure as a catalyst for success and smashing their own imaginary ceilings.

He is the founder and CEO of Maverick Coaching Academy, where he helps fitness professionals build their businesses and make the impact they deserve. He is also working on a solo writing project, *The Conscious Athlete,* where he shares crucial life lessons from his time as an athlete and the stories that forced him to learn them.

Chapter 16

SOCCER–FOREVER MY GUIDING LIGHT

BY KIM BRADY

I'll never forget the day that I fell in love with soccer. I was a little girl, maybe four or five years old, and my brother was playing in an AYSO (The American Youth Soccer Association) game. Since I was so young, I didn't understand the game. My brother was just standing in the back field as a defender—basically, a seven-year-old kid who hated sports and didn't want to chase after the ball, so back then, the coaches just put him on the field.

I had no idea about positions or the rules of the game. Neither did my parents, who simply felt their kids needed to try new activities and sports, so my brother was put into Boy Scouts, tee-ball, soccer, etc. He stayed in Boy Scouts for a while but didn't go all the way to become an Eagle Scout like my dad.

However, he absolutely hated sports, and soccer was not his game. All I knew in that moment was that my brother wasn't chasing after the ball. Therefore, I took it upon myself to run onto the field and chase after it instead, to the horror and embarrassment of my mother and brother, of course, and to the laughter of the other parents on the sidelines.

Thankfully, his coach was wonderful, and he told my mom that I could have a ball to play with on the sidelines so that I wouldn't run back onto the field and interrupt the game. From that moment on, I kept asking if I could play soccer.

I was a tomboy growing up. I ran everywhere. I would ride my bike, climb trees, beat my older brother in races, and I hated wearing dresses. My mom is first-generation Italian, and I was raised with strict gender roles in my family. Girls and women did inside chores such as cooking and cleaning, and the men and boys did outside chores such as mowing the lawn.

Being called a tomboy wasn't necessarily a compliment to me, and even though the name bothered me ("*I am not a boy!*" I would say sometimes when someone said that), I still didn't want to do traditional girly things. I hated dolls and didn't like to do what other girls my age were doing.

My mom even took me to the pediatrician, asking for something to calm me down because I was so hyper and could not sit still. I am beyond grateful that this experience was prior to the craze of giving kids Ritalin and Adderall after being diagnosed with ADHD because instead of drugging me at age six for severe hyperactivity (which I still have), he told my mom to let me play and to keep me physically active.

My parents enrolled me in AYSO the first moment they could. My being prescribed physical activity in order to help me focus is one of my very first recollections of being saved by soccer. At age forty-nine, I can still name every team I have played for, starting with that very first AYSO team called the Rainbows.

From the start, I loved playing the game. I loved that I could get dirty and be physical. I was tiny for my age, and my family had nicknamed me Mighty Mouse because I would not back down from anyone on the field.

In elementary and middle school, I was often picked first for teams, whether we were playing soccer, football, basketball, or any other sport at recess. I rode a BMX bike that my dad helped me put together, and I bought the frame from my brother with my allowance and birthday money.

I also saved up to purchase a ninety-nine-dollar unicycle from the Schwinn bike store not far from my house. I had seen it at the bike shop and immediately fell in love with it. I begged my dad to let me buy it. He told me to save my money, and that if I could save enough, he would let me get it.

Neither of my parents had a clue as to how I was going to ride it, and I often wonder if they thought I wouldn't have the discipline to save my money for it. But sure enough, I saved my money for over six months, and my parents kept their promise. I bought the unicycle, and I also taught myself how to ride it.

My parents put me into gymnastics briefly, but I was too afraid of the balance beam, and I certainly was not graceful or feminine like the other girls were. I hated the leotards, and I didn't have the "all eyes on me" mentality of an individual athlete.

By the time I told my parents I just wanted to play soccer and teach myself how to ride a unicycle, they had learned not to stop me. I became the kid in the neighborhood who rode a unicycle (very well, I might add), a BMX bike, a skateboard, and would dribble a basketball everywhere. But it was soccer that truly had my heart.

By staying active and busy playing outside all the time, I was also a very good student. Physical activity has been linked to improved cognition, and I was proof that medication was not the solution to my hyperactivity. Instead, I needed physical exertion. I loved school, and I enjoyed learning.

The pediatrician had been spot on; my parents kept me active and focused, and I learned the skills necessary to balance my hyperactivity and channel it into healthy results. I liked most of my teachers through elementary school and junior high, and looking back now, junior high was also the start of some of my resourcefulness, my entrepreneurial spirit, and recognizing that I was different from some of my peers.

My junior high school started at 9:05 am, and I was supposed to take the bus to school every day. During seventh grade, I was also expected to ride the bus to an after-school program every day. My parents left for work much earlier than that, and my brother left for high school before I did.

In eighth grade, I no longer had to go to the after-school program, but I was still expected to ride the bus to and from school daily. Instead of taking the bus to school, I would carry my bike down our back hill, out of sight of the neighbors, throw it over the fence, and meet my friend Boyd to ride our bikes via the horse trail to the grocery store before school.

We would buy donut holes and a soda (the healthy breakfast of champions), and then buy twenty-five-cent sodas and a bag of jolly ranchers. I would sell the sodas for a dollar each and sell the individual jolly ranchers for twenty-five cents.

I made bank! Then I proceeded to spend that money every afternoon on arcade games at Lampost Pizza. To this day, I wish I had saved all that money! I am also very lucky my parents had no idea that I had done any of this. I only later shared this story with them as an adult.

They were a bit dismayed, but laughed and said, "Well, that sounds like something you would do. You were very resourceful."

I really wanted to play soccer for the junior high team, and my vice principal even called my mom to advocate for me to play. But my mother was adamant that I go to the after-school program instead. My vice principal recognized how good of an athlete I was, and he also knew how strict my mom was.

But there was no bus to bring me home after the games, and my parents couldn't get out of work in time to pick me up. My mom would never allow me to ride my bike to and from school. It was either ride the bus to the after-school program or ride the bus home.

In eighth grade, I finally got the freedom to come home from school on the bus as a latchkey kid, and I pushed the limit by riding my bike to and from school instead unbeknownst to my parents or brother. In addition to selling soda and candy, I also sold homemade cinnamon toothpicks to my peers.

I ended up getting busted for selling the toothpicks because my classmates would spit them on the floor in class. However, my resourcefulness and entrepreneurial spirit were ignited to find a way around the obstacle, and being told that I couldn't do something made me want to do it more.

Despite not being allowed to play on the junior high school team, I was already playing club/travel soccer. When I was nine, a club coach asked my parents to allow me to play for his team instead of playing for AYSO. I was fast, fearless, and aggressive, and he wanted me on his team.

When my parents asked my thoughts, I said I was afraid, and I didn't think I was good enough to go up a level. Like many young athletes, I played my heart out and was fearless in the moment, but I was extremely insecure and wary of playing on a team with kids who were better than I was.

That was the first of three attempts by this coach to get me to play for him. My parents made me call him directly to tell him that I was declining his offer. They taught me that it was ok to speak directly to my coach and to learn the skills to state what I needed. By age eleven, I was playing club soccer. I was learning how hard being a junior high school kid could be, and I began to see that I was able to play with some of the better players.

It was in junior high that I learned about "mean girls." Some of my teammates would gossip and spread rumors about me or others. I also got into my one and only fistfight with a "friend" who thought I had called her names.

Even when she found out a boy had called her names instead of me, she still spread rumors which led certain girls to not be friends with me. With those not-so-fun experiences to contend with, I chose to move from a recreational team to a club/travel team with the support of the coach who had been recruiting me for the previous three years.

Despite my natural athleticism, I was young, small, and not as physically or mentally mature as other girls in my grade. A lot of my friends were already boy crazy. I tried to jump on the bandwagon by saying I had crushes on boys, but I was only doing it to fit in. The irony was, I fit in even less than I thought. I was a 4.0 GPA student. I was extremely athletic, and a tomboy, and I just wanted to be liked instead of picked on by mean girls. So, I played along, or so I thought.

It was in seventh grade that I was called a lesbian for the first time. In actuality, I believe I was called a dyke, but I have since altered that memory to be less derogatory because I hate that word to this day. I was with my club team members for practice when I reached out to hug a friend, or someone I thought was my friend, but she pushed me away.

She said, "God, you must be a dyke because you are always trying to hug everyone."

I immediately stopped hugging her and didn't say a word. Some of the other girls laughed, and I remember thinking, *okay, no more hugs … and I need to figure out what that word means.* I went home and looked it up in the dictionary. When I read the slang reference, I knew immediately that I never wanted to be called that again. Lesbian lesson 101 in junior high: Don't act like one (whatever "acting like one" means).

I honestly hadn't heard the term before, but I knew it wasn't a good word. I realized then and there what identity I wanted to have, and what I wanted to avoid. I was a soccer player and an athlete, not a tomboy or a dyke.

My identity as Kim the soccer player emerged full force, and my alter ego of being "boy crazy" came in the form of plastering posters of male singers on my walls and talking excitedly about my crushes on boys at school. But never once did I have a boyfriend throughout junior high.

Going into high school at age thirteen and becoming the only freshman on the varsity soccer team was a massive deal. Some of the mean girls on my travel team began to see me as competition on the high school field, and I soon left "the mean girl team" (thankfully).

I became fully engulfed in my varsity team, another travel team, and the Olympic Development Program (ODP). To this day, I am so beyond grateful for those older teammates who took me under their wing as their little sister.

I played on a different club team that was much more welcoming, and I also tried out for ODP as a sophomore. Soccer became my haven and safe place in and outside of school. I won many awards while playing high school soccer from first-team All-League (four years) to MVP of the Freeway League, and our team had three Freeway League Championships.

During this time, I also began to understand my sexuality more. I started dating a boy during junior year. He was a great guy, and we were best friends. He was originally from England, and he also played on the boys' varsity soccer team, but I was not sexually inclined toward him, or any other boy. I could find wonderful qualities about him, but I didn't feel the way my friends felt about their boyfriends. I certainly wasn't having sex, and I am grateful that he never pressured me in any way.

It was while I was dating him that I traveled to Mexico to play on the U16 Cal South ODP team and ultimately met my first love. She played on the U19 team, and I realized for the very first time what my friends meant when they said they had a crush on someone. I remember meeting her on the bus to the fields. She was smart, hilarious, and her laugh was one you could never forget.

She was three years older than me, and I was completely intimidated by her. But still, I couldn't stop thinking about her. I wanted to be near her as often as I could. But I also knew that my feelings were considered unacceptable, and those labels of tomboy and dyke came flooding back. I fell back into appearing straight with my boyfriend and maintaining my identity as a scholar-athlete. Soccer always saved me. I could always rely on it.

I pushed harder to be the best I could be on the soccer field. I tried out for the U19 state team as a sixteen-year-old and didn't make the team. When I walked off the fields after tryouts, my dad asked me how I felt about how I played.

I said, "I don't think I'm good enough, but Julie Foudy (future USWNT player, World Cup Champion, and Olympic Gold Medalist) sat with me and said to keep trying so that means a lot."

I didn't know I was playing against a future World Cup Champion because that wasn't on the radar back then, but I knew that she was one of the best players I had ever seen. I had a long way to go to be able to be as good as her. I continued to play year-round in high school, club, and ODP. I made the state and regional ODP teams my senior year, and I was offered scholarships to play soccer in college.

I kept in contact with my first real crush over those years, and we developed a friendship outside of the ODP teams. She lived in San Diego and could drive, and she would come up to see me as often as possible. We each had a boyfriend, but our feelings for one another were undeniable, yet unspoken.

We never talked about them. Neither of us knew how the other person felt and we both were trying to pass as straight. She also came from a more religious background than me, and I think it was harder for her to reconcile her feelings for a girl, especially one who was younger than her.

When I traveled to France for a student exchange during high school, I tried writing to her often. I missed her dearly and even snuck out to make an international call to her in the middle of the night. I can't imagine the cost of that phone call! The day I came home from my trip was the day she left for college, and I was completely heartbroken because I couldn't see her before she moved.

Although my soccer identity was fully intact at this point, my sexual identity was just emerging. I had a choice between two universities, as two of my state coaches were the college coaches who had offered me the scholarships.

My first school visit and recruiting trip was to UC Santa Barbara. My mom wanted me to go there and be closer to home, and she loved the coach because he could speak five languages, including Italian. Then, I went on my recruiting trip to UC Berkeley.

I had purposefully scheduled this recruiting trip during a game that Cal was to play against St. Mary's, the same school where my first love was playing. I completely surprised her, and she was thrilled that I came to watch her play. But again, neither of us admitted our feelings for one another.

I was just so happy to see her and hug her again. And, the moment I walked onto campus with my dad, one of my former state teammates saw me and yelled at me from across the street, "Kimmi, you better fucking come to this school!"

My dad turned to me and said, "Well, I know where you are going," because he could see I already had close friends in the area.

Between being close to my first love and already having a friend on the Cal team, my dad wasn't wrong. I was going to go to Cal no matter what! Cal felt like my favorite pair of jeans. I felt like I was home. I loved that it was farther away from home than UCSB, and the campus and location were filled with all kinds of new people.

I knew that I would be safe in the arms of my soccer team and that I could be closer to the person I had fallen in love with. I had started going to LGBTQ peer groups with other friends and teammates, unbeknownst to my parents, while still dating my boyfriend. I officially broke up with him once I left for college, and I knew it was a matter of time before I accepted my feelings for my first love.

Within the first two weeks of making the college team, I came out as a lesbian, to myself and to my first crush at age seventeen. She had come to surprise me at my very first game. We talked afterward, and she told me that she was gay and that I was the first person she had fallen in love with, but she never knew how I would take it.

"Well, I am gay, too, and I am in love with you, too," I responded.

Despite this feel-good story, nothing is ever that simple. She and I were never to be a couple, and it was a struggle to manage my feelings for her while she was dating other people. But one thing was for certain: I had made it! I took myself to therapy and began coming out to family and friends.

My identity was complete. I was a scholar-athlete, and I was a lesbian. I was proud to be both, even if I couldn't come out to my mom until many years after. I was secure in who I was, and that is what mattered. I genuinely enjoyed the college experience as an openly gay scholar-athlete.

When I look back at the trajectory of my journey as an elite athlete, I can see that much of it came from a love of sport, and my efforts to love myself. It makes sense that when my life changed abruptly by my departure from the team in my senior year in college, I lost who I was as a person in many ways.

During my senior year, a different coach than the one who recruited me had broken much of the trust of the team, causing several players to leave the year prior. There was a genuine sadness that permeated a once-happy group of players.

To add to this problem, I also experienced a betrayal by not only a teammate but my roommate, who took it upon herself to create a massive rift in the team. She knew if players left, she would be able to take their spot as a starter.

During that year, nine seniors and two freshmen left the team, including me. While I have never regretted choosing my integrity and standing up for my teammates and for my word, I was rocked sideways to leave the game at the peak of my career. I knew that I could never play the game I loved at a higher level than the one I left.

At the time, unless you were on the National Team with Julie Foudy and company, D1 college ball was the highest level a female soccer player could achieve. I knew my career was over. My identity as a soccer player vanished in an instant. I also knew that school was still very important to me, and so I continued on to graduate school. I chose to go very far away, to Michigan and Western Michigan University, where I knew no one and I didn't have to hear about the abrupt end to my soccer career.

> " My identity was complete. I was a scholar-athlete, and I was a lesbian. I was proud to be both "

My first love and I never became girlfriends for various reasons; it was young love, bad timing, not the right person, etc. My heart had been broken by others many times by that point. Going far away felt better than staying.

It was in grad school where people recognized the athlete in me and where I had come from, and a fellow classmate asked me to help coach his daughter's team. Despite my initial desire to keep my soccer career under wraps, I had a graduate assistantship to work at the student recreation center and I was in the gym constantly.

Grad school consisted of small classes, and we all shared a lot about our undergraduate experiences.

Part of the reason I had been accepted into the program was due to my varied experiences as a scholar-athlete, as well as my academics. At age twenty-one, I realized that even if I couldn't play anymore, maybe I could still be a part of the game. My classmate told me to get the state coaching license, which I did, and that was the catalyst for me getting two additional national licenses with the thought of coaching collegiately at some point.

This began a fourteen-year career coaching girls' soccer while trying to figure out what to do with my life. I coached girls' teams ages thirteen to eighteen, and also was an assistant coach to a U14 boys ODP team.

In 2002, I moved to Colorado and continued coaching teams there for a few years until my schedule changed and I couldn't continue. The ability to reinvent myself wasn't by choice, but out of necessity, based on the need for more income and financial stability in a career. Unfortunately, coaching didn't cover the bills.

In addition to coaching, I became an outspoken advocate for LGBTQ rights. I spoke on panels, coached soccer part-time, and became a registered social worker (RSW) for the state of Michigan, and I was a marital and family therapist by the young age of twenty-five. I began working with abused and neglected youth at age twenty-two while still in school, and once I got my master's, I worked with kids and families from all walks of life.

It was then that I finally reached out to my parents to thank them for all of their years of love and sacrifice to pay for my years of soccer. I was so grateful that I had not grown up the way some of the kids I worked with did.

When I was twenty-nine, I left Michigan and the counseling world behind. I couldn't do it anymore. My last client experience was to administer first aid to a sixteen-year-old girl who had attempted suicide. It was just too much for me to manage emotionally. I'd had it with the therapy world, with being in the muck of people's minds. The damage that I witnessed done to children was more than I could handle. I left the counseling field and my seven and a half years of schooling.

Once again, everything I had known was gone. I had to start over again. I had pivoted from my identity as an athlete to one of being a therapist, and that too had been stripped away in a moment. I moved to Colorado and decided that since I had a "people degree," I could figure out a job. I knew I needed to learn how to make money because coaching and therapy don't pay well at all! I was broke, in debt from grad school, and working multiple jobs to still be broke, mentally and financially. I thought sales might be a good fit.

I spent the next several years hopping between sales positions, always going after the next big thing, and thinking the grass would be greener at another company. I would stay at one company for two or three years and then want to leave for various reasons. I could never find "my favorite pair of jeans," and none of the jobs I worked felt like the right fit. I worked crazy hours and couldn't continue coaching soccer.

I chased dollars but never broke the six-figure mark, despite my best efforts and being in the top ten or twenty percent of salespeople at every company I was a part of.

Finally, after going home to California to visit my nephew, I realized I was chasing something that didn't exist. I was trying to find an identity in a corporate suit that felt foreign. I decided I needed to walk my walk and be a good example for my nieces and nephews. I had pursued my dreams, but I was miserable, and my nephew recognized it.

When I was chatting with him about his future plans, he said, "Aunt Kim, you have always supported me and have always followed your dreams. But right now, you're miserable and I am having a hard time wanting to follow your advice."

I knew I needed to walk my talk to my nieces and nephews because they looked up to me. So, I quit. *Again.* I spent the next few weeks formulating the decision to not only build a company but to also invite my nephew to come live with me.

So many people think it's risky to become an entrepreneur and to build a business. What was risky for me was continuing to chase a nine-to-five job and pursue the goals of other people while not knowing what mine were anymore. I was completely miserable in my corporate position, and I knew I had to stop running and find myself again. I needed to tap into a place I had locked up for a while: the soccer player in me and the little entrepreneur of my childhood.

I have always lived to the beat of my own drum in many ways. I had been the only one of my high school friends to get an athletic scholarship to college. Since I had zero experience with business, I tapped into the only thing I knew best: soccer and how to build a team.

I didn't care that we were in the middle of a recession in 2010. I didn't care that my financial advisor told me to scrap my first idea of a coffee shop. She knew that my idea of a coffee shop and "bringing California to Denver" wasn't my real dream. She knew that I really wanted to move back home to California, and a brick-and-mortar coffee shop would only anchor me in a place I didn't want to be.

So, I needed to take the time to figure out a business that would allow me to eventually move back home to California and the ocean. I didn't listen to people who told me how crazy it was to have my nephew come live with me. Just as I had taught myself how to ride a unicycle as a child, and as I pursued soccer with a fervor that got me to the highest level, I was going to build a company.

I was going to do it my way. I knew that I thrived with good coaching and great managers, and I knew what kind of coaching I hated. I didn't want to be that kind of leader. I went after building my business the way you build a soccer team.

I found good coaches and advisors, I surrounded myself with people who were bigger, better, faster, and stronger than me, and then I went to work. Every day, for ten years, I exhibited complete devotion to building my company, TEAMLBC.

One of my nicknames in soccer had been Little Bit, and that became the name of my company: Little Bit Cleaning LLC®. When I hired my first employees, "me" became "we." Once we had a crew of people, I referred to them as TEAMLBC. Every team and business has people who assume different roles. In soccer, you need captains, subs, and different positions, and the same is true in business. I needed my part-time folks, my full-time folks, my coaches, and my manager.

Aside from soccer, being a business owner has been my longest career. I came to it naturally, just like I did with soccer, and I am forever continuing to learn. I sold my company two days before lockdown due to Covid, and now I help former athletes build their small businesses as a business coach. From the soccer field to the business playing field, I love the game.

Soccer has taught me to be relentless in my pursuits, act as a team player, and remain disciplined in the face of adversity. It has taught me to work through life's difficulties and capitalize on my strengths. The internal drive that I had as an athlete transferred directly to business ownership. I will always be an athlete in mindset and purpose, and soccer was and will always be my first love.

It's a blessing to pay it forward in other ways as an entrepreneur, and I have come full circle from where I started. I moved back to Southern California, sold my first company, and started my own business coaching company. I have gotten back into coaching on the soccer field as well, with a U-16 team back in the same county where I ran onto my brother's field at the age of four. Whenever anyone asks how I built my business, I just tell them that "soccer made me," and taught me everything I need to know about building my company.

As a developing soccer player, I constantly sought out better coaching and teams, and the same was true when it came to my journey as a business owner. I chose coaches and advisors who would help me retain that leading edge in my business. I built a team of people around me and created a support system of advisors that helped when times became hard and celebrated with me when we had small and big wins. I picked "captains" and had employees "on the bench" ready to go, and we created a team mentality that allowed for true friendship both at work and in life.

Soccer will always be my guiding light, and I am forever grateful for the gifts it has brought to me and continues to bring. Being a Forever Athlete is about carrying your passions and purpose forward, and in my case, on and off the field, in business and in life. I am honored to help athletes transition from their sport and into business, just as I did.

My current status as a business coach is the culmination of my varied career path as an athlete, therapist, salesperson, business owner, and entrepreneur. I am also still coaching soccer and paying it forward to other kids with big dreams.

I am a keynote speaker who talks about entrepreneurship, LGTBQ+ issues, and the sometimes-rocky transition from sport to career. My hope is to teach others to love the game as much as I did, and to provide a path for them to be successful on and off the field in whatever way they choose.

ABOUT KIM

Kim Brady is the entrepreneur, keynote speaker, author, and business coach behind Kim Brady Business Coaching. She can help you orchestrate the blueprint of your life and business on your own terms. Her areas of expertise include small business start-ups, the transition from sports, team building, leadership development, and LGBTQ+ advocacy.

Kim is also a former marriage and family therapist specializing in working with severely abused children. She is a former four-year D1 scholarship recipient for women's soccer at Cal Berkeley and has coached youth soccer for fourteen years. She is the founder and former president of Little Bit Cleaning LLC® located in Denver, Colorado, which she successfully sold in 2020 after ten years of ownership.

Her energy and enthusiasm to help others succeed and achieve their goals both on and off the athletic field are unmatched. Kim has a passion for learning and believes that just because we no longer compete in our sport does not mean we have to lose that athletic mindset to build a business or create the future we desire.

Kim is the author of *Get Stuck In!* (available for purchase on her website and on Amazon), and she is taking on new clients for her coaching practice and scheduling keynote speaking engagements. Reach out to her to schedule an initial consult or to schedule an event.

Connect with Kim:
Website: www.kimbradybusinesscoaching.com
LinkedIn: https://www.linkedin.com/in/kimbrady/
Instagram: @coachkb15
Clubhouse: @coachkb1516
Facebook: coachkb15
Twitter: coachkb15

Chapter 17

NO LONGER THE VICTIM
BY SARAH WILLIAMS

"Be who you were born to be, not what the world has transformed you to become."

— Sarah Williams

Some people are born gifted, while others simply try to find a way to survive. Talent isn't always natural, though it can be created. I wasn't always an athlete. Instead, I adopted an athletic identity in order to escape abuse.

My childhood was one of chaos, turmoil, and trauma. While growing up, my home was not a place of peace, love, and comfort. Instead, it was one of pain, rage, and suffering. I had a stepfather who dominated the household and everyone in it in every way. I felt as if I was a piece of property that was owned. If I didn't do what he said, then there would be hell to pay.

This hell consisted of mental, physical, emotional, and sexual abuse. The home I grew up in felt like more of a prison. There were so many times that I was locked in my room, grounded from anything but school, and received beatings that should have put that man in prison himself. These instances didn't only happen to me; my siblings endured even worse cruelty than I did.

Participating in sporting events gave me a sense of community, hope, and support that I wasn't given at home. It was the purpose I needed to survive. Had I not become an athlete, I believe I wouldn't be here today, and I would not be able to call myself a survivor.

"
Talent isn't always natural, though it can be created.
"

While you are putting all your effort into surviving day-to-day, you can't dream. I started doing well in sports after becoming an athlete, and I started getting noticed. I chose athletics because it was easily available in school, and my parents supported this choice if I could provide the transportation, extra financial demands, and keep grades up and home chores, which I did.

I had created an identity that I liked better than the reality I was living. I realized I enjoyed being recognized. I also loved winning because it provided the confidence boost I needed. At that point in my life, I started to dream bigger. I wanted to do better, be better, and try to become the best.

At the age of eight, hope was not a concept I was familiar with. The first time I experienced it was when I started my first sport as an equestrian. The first horse I leased was named Shadow. She was not a horse of perfect confirmation. Her posture was not all square; she was a bit different, in the best way.

She had long ears that laid flat, side to side, which earned her the nickname of "Airplane." At our 4H fair fun night, we even decorated her like an airplane. We built long wings out of cardboard that went over my saddle, and I wore an aviator hat, glasses, and a scarf, which I like to think gave me an incredible resemblance to Amelia Earhart.

My relationship with Shadow showed me love, trust, and commitment in a safe environment where I began to experience joy while working hard for what I wanted to accomplish. There is something about the soul connection between a horse and a human that is deeply healing. The sense of pride I took in my accomplishments radiated throughout my entire being, and I noticed a faint smile start to appear on my face.

Shadow and I became best friends; we had formed a bond that could not be broken. She let me cry on her shoulder when I needed to escape the pain, and she met me with loving compassion that only my grandmother had been able to give me.

When we loped through the cornfields with my long, dark hair flying in the wind, I felt free. That was all I wanted to be—free from pain, fear, rejection, abuse, and the life I couldn't leave. It was during this time that I realized I could accomplish anything I set my mind to.

Every dream begins with a dreamer. Being an athlete helped me develop critical life skills like perseverance, tenacity, discipline, work ethic, standing up for myself, and using my own voice. These life skills allowed me to achieve competitive goals like such as a lifetime award-winning equestrian, 2016 Top 10 Age Group Triathlete, 2017 Age Group Champion Pacific Northwest Triathlete, 2017 National Championship Duathlete, and 2018 World Qualifying Duathlete.

I continued my journey as an equestrian athlete throughout middle and high school, as well as participating in multiple other sports. Every sport I was involved in meant less time at home, which was my first dream to accomplish. However, it was not that simple. I came from a very poor household, consisting of five kids and two adults, and being the oldest girl automatically put me in a position to be the caretaker.

While my mom worked, I was responsible for most of the household chores, which included preparing food for the family. I found myself being quite creative when it came to making several meals out of the same ingredients.

While all five of us kids wanted to participate in something to be out of the home, money was not in the cards for all of us to join a sport. This meant it was up to me to find ways to make money, starting at age twelve, to pay for my personal things including toiletries and school sports fees. I started by taking in cans and bottles, babysitting, working in berry fields, weeding onion fields in the hot sun, and any other type of work I could find.

When it came time to purchase the equipment and gear to participate, I had to opt for what myself and my parents could afford, which was far from the latest and greatest. I used the same shoes for multiple years, hoping they would fit. I wore hand-me-downs, and if they were new, they were "pro-wings"—a notoriously cheap brand—which I got teased for wearing.

Comparison and despair started to take a deep hold in my ability to perform. I started to believe that if I didn't have Nike shoes, I couldn't run as fast as my peers. If I didn't have the cute shorts the other girls did, I was sure I wouldn't be able to clear the high hurdles. That was how I felt; somehow, other people having better gear automatically meant they were better than me.

I knew I had to fight hard to prove to myself that I belonged. I felt I had to work harder to not let the doubt creep in and ruin my ability to achieve my dreams. I was no stranger to hard work; my life was entirely hard work.

The idea of perfectionism was one I consumed wholeheartedly. If I didn't have the best gear, then I had to be the best of the best to win. This didn't stop with sports; the idea of being perfect or the best of the best at anything meant my identity had to change. I became a model student, star employee, and worked hard to perform as well as I could in everything I set my mind to.

I started receiving recognition, appreciation, and encouragement, which told me that I was being noticed. It was exactly what I had always wanted. The positive reinforcement I received when I accomplished one of my goals was something I became addicted to. I realized quickly that excelling in sports was an outlet to get what I so desperately craved at home.

While it is true that most of us can't be good at everything, I have learned that we can get better at what we focus on. Sports became an opportunity to escape my home situation physically, though I was never gone emotionally. I left home at age seventeen and continued a relationship with a man nine years older who had the cutest one-and-a-half-year-old daughter. I was naïve as I believed I could escape the emotional pain by hoping someone else could rescue me. I later married this man and gained a beautiful daughter.

During my marriage, I became the vision of what I thought a perfect wife was, though I found it extremely difficult as I carried scenes from my childhood into adulthood. These actions included sweeping things under the rug that should have been dealt with, walking on eggshells not to disrupt the family, avoiding conflict, pretending everything was perfect, and I definitely was not nurturing. In fact, I was quite controlling.

I wasn't the perfect wife or mother. I wanted to be loving, caring, supportive, and the opposite of what I had experienced in my childhood, but I knew, deep down, I had failed. It ate me up inside. I was living what I had learned; to suffer was normal, and abuse of all kinds was acceptable to give and receive, which was not a safe place for me or my family to exist. I began to realize I was repeating a cycle that I had never actually healed. I later divorced my husband and did what I knew best: I leaned back into sports.

The fastest way to make myself feel better was to throw myself wholly into being an athlete once again. I started to go to the gym, attend classes, and participate in races for fun. It quickly became an obsession for me, as did being conscious of everything I put into my body. This athletic mindset felt like an old soft shoe—so comfortable, recognizable, and familiar. I felt at home, which, to me, meant I was not at home.

I again became addicted to the energy I got from making new friends, being recognized, and being noticed. Thus, my new life began. During the next few years, I was introduced to triathlons, something I never expected to become involved in. I remember my cousin, Craig, stating he had done a triathlon, and this guy was probably 300 pounds and around six feet tall.

He was the one who, at Christmas and family dinners, made fun of the way I was eating because it was much healthier than the abundance of Oreos and milk he was bragging about devouring in one sitting. I knew that if he could complete a triathlon, surely, I could as well. I can still hear the little voice inside my head that piped up when the opportunity came along: *challenge accepted.*

The race that Craig chose to participate in was only three weeks away at that time, in the beginning of April in Oregon. My triathlon career started in 2013 with the Beaver Freezer race. Some might ask why it is called the Beaver Freezer, and my answer to you would be because you freeze your rear end off. Immediately upon leaving the pool after the half-mile swim, you begin to ride your bike twelve miles (in the rain and wind, in my case) while soaking wet.

All this, only to find yourself running your three-mile course as if you had cement blocks tied to your feet. To say it was freezing cold is putting it politely.

Here is where my story turns a little humorous. I did not know how to swim competitively. I loved water, and still do, but putting my face down in the water while swimming was very foreign to me. Did I also mention I had only ridden a bike a handful of times since I was a child? I had bought a bike from a friend just weeks before to try something new. After my maiden ten-mile voyage on the bike, my booty hurt so badly I was afraid I had made the wrong choice about buying that bike.

I was not afraid of the running portion. Somehow, after all those years, I still had it as far as running goes. I was learning two new sports at once and putting three sports together in one competition, and I had no idea how to train for it. All I knew was that I had three weeks to learn how to swim while keeping my face in the water, as well as attempt to ride a road bike on the streets in the pouring rain where it gets dark at five o'clock and survive.

By the time of the race, I had quite a few people rooting for me, and it felt great. This is when I learned that once you're an athlete, you're always an athlete. Just because I had a break in my athletic career didn't mean I no longer possessed the physical and mental ability.

That triathlon was by far the most difficult challenge I had ever undertaken as an athlete, and I successfully completed it. The memory of that day will forever be imprinted in my mind, as it was one of the best days of my life.

Not only did I complete the challenge (with only a minor hiccup— my arms were so tired it took me a few tries to get out of the pool), but I had my very own fan club of friends and family that showed up with the most support I had ever received during a sporting event. This was a surprise that I wasn't expecting, and it was one of the greatest surprises I've ever received.

I finished the race ahead of Craig, and that was all that really mattered! That race was where I learned to push my body, and I wanted more. What else could I do? The body, as a machine, became so impressive to me. All the worries that had plagued me before were far from my mind. I became laser-focused on becoming the best triathlete I could.

The first year and a half were a blur consisting of race after race on almost every weekend, starting in April or May. The race calendar Craig put together left no time for anything but work and training. Throughout the seasons, I not only found a new passion, but I found a community. Triathletes are some of the most humbling people I know. We became a group of something which I would like to call "the suffer club."

We would talk about each other's pain caves and grueling runs, hill repeats, who had the most climbing on their bike rides, strength workouts, boring swim workouts, and so much more. They became my new tribe. The true friends I met during this phase of life have been some of the greatest people to challenge my growth as an athlete and as a human. Training for and racing triathlons became my new addiction. The more I worked at it, the more I wanted to do, and the better I wanted to become.

I eventually hired an amazing coach to help me reach new goals and learn so much about my body. Indeed, I was a top-performing athlete once again, and I knew I could do whatever I set my mind to. I couldn't wait to excel at new workouts so I could complete them and analyze the data. It was fascinating to see how much of a machine my body had become.

I held this schedule until 2014, at which point I wanted to be a bit more competitive in the pool, and so I asked a friend to help me learn flip turns. Flip turns, I had heard, could shave a few seconds off your swim time on each end of the pool. After one lesson in the pool with my friend showing me how to do these turns, I decided I was ready to do it on my own.

I went to my local pool and couldn't wait to put my new tricks to work. I got in, did my warmup, and decided it was time to give it a try. I pushed off the wall, made it to the deeper end and completed a flip turn. I swam back and tried it again on the shallow end, very cautiously, I might add. I continued this pattern for maybe 100 yards. I pushed off the wall once again, made it to the deep end, and started swimming back toward the shallow end.

This flip turn did not go as expected. In fact, it changed my life forever. I pushed off the wall with all the strength in my legs, but I must have pushed a bit too hard. I was unable to complete the rotation underwater, and the back of my head hit the bottom of the stone-cold, hard concrete pool. With all the power and force that the largest muscles in my body could produce, my head took a direct hit.

I don't remember losing consciousness, though I do remember popping up and hoping that no one had witnessed my awful display of a flip turn. I continued to swim for a few moments, but it must have been adrenaline keeping me going at that point because dizziness and nausea overtook me as soon as I hit the deep end. I thought it might be wise to exit the pool and call it a day. I had rationalized the nausea and dizziness to simply mean I may not have eaten enough to sustain my work out that day.

I'd had concussions before, most of them due to horse-related injuries. The thought that I could have a concussion was in the back of my mind, but I buried it deep because I didn't want to stop competing. I drove straight from the pool to my mother-in-law's house and collapsed on the floor, only to get up to vomit in the toilet. I still thought that it was because I hadn't eaten enough. So, I mentioned to her my little swimming accident and headed for home.

I called my partner at the time, who was working nights, and described what had happened. I asked them to wake me up when the workday was done. My partner did not make it home before I had to leave for work, but luckily, I awoke from my alarm. I got ready and headed to work like nothing had happened. I arrived at work around 6:30 am, sat at my computer, and did my morning tasks. My computer screen started appearing blurry, and my ears were ringing. Soon, a headache started.

I remember sitting in a meeting with the president and vice president of the company. I started to get very hot, sweaty, nauseated, and I stared blankly like I was watching the meeting from above. I wasn't mentally there, and I removed my sweater, which was very unusual for me as I'm always cold.

At that time, I think people started to become concerned about me. They were asking me questions, but I couldn't hear them; it was like I was somewhere else. I was taken to the hospital and diagnosed with a concussion.

This was the beginning of another downfall in my life. I was sent home to rest for three days in the dark and instructed to follow up with my primary care physician. After the three days were up, I did not feel any better, so off to the doctor I went. It was another five to seven days in the dark for me. It went on like this for a month or two with no real improvement. Of course, I couldn't work, I wasn't training, and I started to feel hopeless and depressed.

Finally, a light bulb went on in my brain and I thought, *Sarah, you know how to get out of this.* Just like any other laser-focused athlete, I put on my running shoes and headed out the door. *This concussion isn't going to get me down,* I decided, *I am going to train through it.* When I was exercising, I would feel clarity in my mind again. I could think for a few minutes as the fog lifted and the light returned. When I wasn't training, the thoughts that crept into my mind were some of the most debilitating thoughts I have ever had.

Why do bad things always seem to happen to me?
Haven't I been through enough? I guess this is just how my life is.
Life was meant to be hard; good things were not meant to happen to me.

My self-worth was low, I had no job, I was depressed, and I couldn't remember anything. I was frustrated. My community had moved on without me; my support system couldn't help me, as I couldn't communicate what was wrong exactly or what I needed from them. I had never felt so alone since I was a child.

After not seeing overall improvement after a doctor's appointment, I was told I had to rest or I wouldn't ever recover. My partner locked my shoes, bike tire, and other items in the safe so I couldn't train.

There was a time during this period where I did try to take my own life. Month after month, I had little improvement. I had a team of doctors, a concussion clinic, a sports psychologist, a counselor, and my regular doctor overseeing my case. No one could explain why I wasn't seeing improvement, and the only data I had was that when I was training, I felt better.

I wasn't the same person as before the concussion. I lost everything I had worked so hard for. I was numb—no joy, no hope, just existing.

Everything seemed out of my control, I was not even able to be a contributing member of society. I eventually went back to work ten months after the original injury, though it wasn't the same position. I had been a program manager for our number two customer in our company prior to leaving. Upon return, my position was to work two hours a day counting parts in the stockroom.

That somehow didn't seem fair, and it bruised my ego pretty badly. I didn't understand at the time, but this was a business decision, not one that discredited me as a person. Within the next two months, I worked hard to get back the job I'd once had, and I was successful. That boosted my spirits a bit, but I wasn't happy.

It wasn't until 2016 to 2017 that I somehow crawled out of the despair I had faced during my concussion and returned strong to the racing scene. I ended up racing some of the best races in my life in 2017. I won multiple awards, many races, and I qualified for world events, where the best of the best athletes from all over the world compete.

In fact, I was an age-group champion in 2017. I was so excited to have finally proved to myself that my hard work was paying off. I felt brave, so I gave myself another challenge, this time a full marathon.

This goal, unfortunately, was very short-lived; on one of my training hikes, I experienced an incredible amount of pain in my calf. I was hiking around Hagg lake, and there was only one way back to the car. I had to go around it. I was in so much pain I almost thought about hitching a ride from some random stranger to my car. As a single lady out in the middle of nowhere, with no cell phone service, I decided to tough it out.

Every step I took was followed by excruciating pain, and I had no idea what had happened. The only goal was to get back to my car. I finally made it, headed home, and looked at my calf. I saw what looked like the biggest bruise I had ever seen on my body. The next morning, I couldn't walk, which meant a trip to the emergency room once again. An exam and the MRIs confirmed I had torn a muscle in my calf, which meant my marathon training had to be postponed for another year.

In February of 2018, I started losing feeling in my right arm. It was going numb, tingling, and incredibly painful from my neck and down through my arm. I went to the doctor for an MRI and found out that two discs in my neck were herniated and pressing on my spinal column, causing all the pain. I then learned I had to have surgery to replace two disks in my neck, which meant that I was unable to compete in the world competition.

That was another dream of mine crushed by something that was out of my control. All that hard work, training, suffering, and sacrifice now felt like it was for nothing. Injuries do happen, and I'm aware of this. I've had my share, but this? It didn't feel fair. The same day I had my spinal surgery, my grandma passed away. She was the one person in the world who I knew loved me wholeheartedly.

We had an undeniable connection that kept me alive in my darkest times. She was my favorite person on the Earth, and this was an unexpected loss that I was unprepared for. My heart had never been so shattered; this was suffering I was not trained to deal with. Later that year, I had to have another surgery. I just couldn't seem to catch a break. 2018 was one of the hardest years I have endured, and I didn't know if I would ever be the athlete I could be.

It was during this time that the Sarah I knew became very lost. My entire identity, formed around my athleticism, was gone. Again, I had lost my community, my training partners, and racing, which provided what I thought was happiness. I had lost a relationship and people who loved me. I had lost friends and became completely unavailable to anyone. I did not know who I was without sports.

Since 2014, I have had three more concussions. I have had a total of eight concussions in my life, all with different capacities that have changed my brain and the way I function. It was very easy to fall into a victim mentality.

This just doesn't happen to regular people. It only happens to me.

This is where the work gets even harder, and this work is not physical. It is mental.

I couldn't run away from the pain deep within my soul any longer. Everything I had tried to escape all those years flooded right back to the forefront once participating in sports was no longer an option. I began to realize I had felt better physically through sports, but the emotional pain I was running from had gone unhealed. I had to change my lifestyle if I wanted to preserve what brain capacity I had left.

Part of this change also meant that I could no longer have my horse, and an equestrian was something I had always been. I honestly didn't know who I was without a horse.

All I saw were the bad things that kept happening to me, and I thought it would always be that way. I had my share of tests, I became exhausted, and I didn't understand what lesson I was supposed to learn. Going back to triathlons is something that I may do again someday, though I know I won't be competing at the same level, as it is not safe for me to do so. I am not the person I was before the injuries, and it is something I had to face to heal. This is another painful reality check that tells me I am not invincible.

One day, I said these few words to myself: "I am no longer a victim."

These words changed my life instantly. I started to tap back into my values and discover who I really was on a soul level, face my problems head-on, and learn that I have a choice. I chose to learn the lesson in all those cases of disappointment, and what I learned is that I cannot run away and cover up what's bothering me with something outside of myself.

The blame game had to stop. It wasn't my mom's fault. It wasn't my childhood. It wasn't that I was handed a deck of bad cards. It was simply because I was playing the victim role in my own life on repeat.

It was my fault for allowing those events to take up so much negative space in my life. I didn't have my own back on all levels, and I wanted to know why. I was so comfortable in this role in my life that anything outside my "normal" felt like a threat, and I ran from anything that could possibly be good in my life.

If something did start to go well, I sure as hell would sabotage it because, somehow, I knew good things were not meant for me. Instead of getting my hopes up, I would ruin any possibility of anything going the way I wanted it to.

I just couldn't wrap my brain around why I did this, so I decided to dive into some deep work that forced me to look in the mirror and face things I had never been able to see before. I asked myself two questions:

1. Is what I am thinking about myself true and factual?
2. What am I making it mean?

This is where everything started to click; I needed to learn how to like myself for who I was. I recognized the people-pleaser within me and understood that the only person I needed to please was staring back at me in that mirror. This is where I began to connect with my identity of who I am at the core.

I had become whomever I needed to be to survive, and being an athlete was hard, so I was able to focus so much energy and rage into being productive on the course. As I began to peel away the layers of hard stone that built the walls surrounding me for protection, I started seeing a very vulnerable woman who didn't even love herself. I am so much more than all the bad things that have happened to me.

The fire was lit, and I was going all-in on myself! I realized that I couldn't wait until life wasn't hard anymore to be happy.

I then became intentional about what I would give my energy to, and I chose healing. This work I committed to has been hands down the hardest, yet most fulfilling, work I have ever done. A beautiful shift started happening within me. Instead of seeking all the negative in each situation, I started to focus on what went well, what I enjoyed, and what the experience taught me. I started the practice of forgiveness and gratitude, and that provided a lot of peace within me.

I focused more on living from a place that aligned with my morals and values by leading with love, compassion for myself and others, and integrity.

This put me in alignment to become the highest version of myself. I had found my true identity, which was there all along; I just didn't know to access it through all the pain. I now felt peace for the first time in my life, and I knew I couldn't keep this breakthrough to myself. Pain, purpose, and hope can co-exist, and I am now living my ultimate purpose: fulfilling my passion by helping others discover their true identity.

My role in the athlete world may have changed, but I am just as committed as I ever was during my playing days. Through all the craziness my life has been, I not only survived, but I excelled. I have discovered a passion and purpose that is far greater than what I could have found as simply a competitor.

I now help athletes from all over the world learn that they are so much more than the sport they play. I am an athletic identity coach that helps athletes learn who they are when they are not playing and prepare them for life's adversity on and off the field.

As athletes, our careers are very short-lived, and I want to help as many people as I can to not go through what I did. So many of the athletes I have helped said they wished they had someone like me before they faced career-ending injuries or contracts not being renewed. Because of my experience, I am now living the best life I have ever lived. It is possible to have it all, even after your athletic career is over.

Once an athlete, always an athlete.

Since being on the other side of my journey of participating in athletics, I have learned so many amazing things about myself. The athlete inside me never died just because of an injury and career cut too short. Being a forever athlete doesn't mean you have to compete your entire lifetime; to me, it means that I take what I have learned and repurpose it to help others excel at their sport for the rest of my life. My goals for the athlete I want to become are now different, but they are not viewed as less important.

Life ebbs and flows, and we must take the good with the bad. The biggest thing that has come from my stepping down from racing is being able to embrace my true identity, using skills like tenacity, respect, deep-rooted strength, and passion to pass what I have learned to others.

I currently own a coaching practice where I work one-on-one with athletes to help them become successful in life, on and off the field, by helping them identify who they truly are. Once they have identified who they really are by diving deep within their own values, the mindset starts to shift for the better. Having a more thorough mental awareness of self will directly show in the results on and off the field. In stepping down from competing, I have stepped up my purpose.

It is when you can take the most pain you've encountered in your life and turn it into a purpose, by giving hope and inspiration to others, that you know you have discovered your superpower.

I am the hero of my story now and help others become the same in theirs. Remember, you always have a choice: Become the victim or be the hero of your own journey.

ABOUT SARAH

Sarah Williams spends most of her time in northwest Oregon, where she was born and raised. While she has faced many challenges throughout her life, she has learned that tenacity and perseverance have always prevailed when getting through the darkest of days. Sarah is a multi-sport athlete who has endured her share of injuries, recoveries, and loss of identity when faced with multiple traumatic brain injuries.

Sarah not only practices what she preaches but has always had a special gift of connecting with others on the deepest levels. She is the founder of Born to Endure athletic identity coaching, where she helps other athletes learn to face adversity and discover they are more than the sport they play. She works with athletes of many disciplines all over the world to become who they are meant to be at their core.

Sarah is professionally trained and certified and has helped her clients be who they were born to be, not what the world has transformed them to become. When her players become mentally aligned with who they truly are at their core, their performance on and off the field is extraordinary. Whether you are still competing, recovering from injury, or retiring and finding your next career, your success is directly related to your mental wellbeing. Sarah has overcome so much in her life, but her biggest challenge was to learn she is no longer a victim.

Connect with Sarah:
Website: www.borntoendure.com
Email: sarah@borntoendure.com
Instagram: @borntoendure.coaching

Chapter 18

YOU DICTATE THE SCORE

BY KEEGAN LAMAR

Every game comes to an end. Whether the game is a career-defining competition, a major phase of life, or just practice, every one has a natural conclusion. When that time comes, there is a score that will forever be written in stone, capturing far more than surface-level points.

It will capture the heart you displayed to go the distance when times were challenging, the stories you used to push far past your limits, the physical preparation to compete unhindered when you were the underdog, and the number of people you inspired through the way you carried yourself.

That score will also expose your lack of interest when conditions weren't ideal. It will display the excuses you leaned on to validate mediocrity, highlight the laziness in your training when you didn't want to push yourself, and tally the number of people who began to believe that it doesn't take much to be an athlete.

This scoreboard reflects the person you are, not the person you believe yourself to be. If you are walking the talk, the score will reflect it. If you half-ass your way through the trials and challenges, that, too, will be reflected.

People believe that great stats and an impeccable record indicate who the champions are in this world. However, I believe that those are simply byproducts of someone who puts the lifestyle of a champion into everything they do each day.

The accolades and statistics simply reflect the person you already are. You always have a champion within you, ready to take the stage and thrive; that internal champion is your potential. The results we pursue are always specific to the game we are playing.

However, the methods you use to achieve those results will remain consistent and unique to how you operate best. Your ability to get the results you desire is called performance. Therefore, your performance is determined by your ability to tap into your total potential.

To make it simple, performance = potential – distractions.

Your potential is everything within you that is designed to help you succeed in the game you're playing. Distractions are everything that do not serve you in getting the results you want in life right now. They pull your time, attention, and energy away from your potential.

What do Michael Jordan, Michael Phelps, Tom Brady, Serena Williams, and Usain Bolt all have in common? They all can take over a competition in an instant.

They all embody the phrase "It's not over till it's over," and their accomplishments speak for themselves.

Every so often, an athlete comes along that just seems to have a superpower where they can choose if they want to win at a moment's notice. These kinds of athletes demand our attention, and we can all feel their electricity when they compete. It's one of the most amazing things to watch as a fan, and, for an athlete, being in the zone often feels like an out-of-body experience.

What most people don't realize is that, when someone takes over a game, they already had that potential inside of them. Their dedication to being the best comes from being non-negotiable in the goals they set.

This allows these individuals to play at a higher level than most because they can tap into their fullest potential more frequently than others and compete free from distractions. This freedom gives people the ability to get whatever they want, whenever they desire it. The realization that we can command the outcome of the game we play has been the greatest lesson in my life's journey thus far.

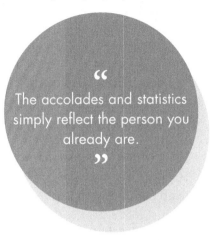

"
The accolades and statistics simply reflect the person you already are.
"

For most of us, this moment generally comes in the midst of an existential crisis, and the need to survive kicks in. Think about the last time you felt like things really hit the fan in your world.

You probably started to wonder, *Why is this happening to me?* Or, you might be thinking, *Here we go again; this always happens.* You might have questioned whether any effort was worth trying to save the situation.

That is when a small flame ignites within, along with the sense of panic that it's either now or never, and never isn't an option. Once this decision is made, a sense of clarity washes over you like a tidal wave, giving you superhuman abilities to move mountains in your world and make life happen for you. You needed change like you needed your next breath of air.

You stepped into the flames, and, no matter what pain you were going to endure, you understood the mission at hand and would not cease until the objective was complete. These moments aren't always dire situations to the outside world, but I guarantee they feel dire to you.

For me, that moment came when I was sitting in traffic. I was heading into a job that I couldn't stand and felt like I was going to throw up.

Instead, I said aloud, "What the hell am I doing?"

I began to hyperventilate, sweat, and felt like I needed to pull over before I slammed on the gas in bumper-to-bumper traffic. I had never felt so lost and misaligned with the person I believed I could be, and it had to change.

That moment hit me like a ton of bricks. I knew I was meant for more. I needed to discover what my true potential was, how I could harness it, and how it would serve the world. But, to do that, I had to understand that I wasn't dictating the score in my life, and I was the only one who possessed the responsibility and ability to change that.

I'm grateful for that moment because it has gifted me the opportunity to share my experiences with you. I hope my experience allow you to skip the in-traffic crisis I had.

We all get to choose how we approach our unique performance formulas to tilt the score in our favor. We decide the results we wish to experience, the parts of our potential that serve us best in seeing those results, and how we want to mitigate distractions from pulling us away from that potential.

You know the price you must pay to get what you want, but you're unwilling to pay it. You also know all the distractions that are currently plaguing your life, but you haven't done anything about them. An athletic mindset always looks to increase potential but has a hard time removing distractions, even though we all know they take away from our ability to get the results we wish to see.

Why is this?

To put it simply, we all want to look in the mirror when we know we'll like what we see. It's those moments when we are willing to look in the mirror, despite knowing that the person looking back makes us sick or disappointed, that we unlock the moments that will change the way we compete forever.

Athletes are conditioned to present themselves as wearing a coat of armor that is bulletproof in all ways. I challenge you to take a new approach and embrace vulnerability. The more vulnerable you are, the more you will grow and become bulletproof. Your armor must be made with transparent steel.

I never wanted to look in the mirror throughout my athletic career. Even today, I still have trouble taking the time to look at myself. When I was an athlete, I often saw fear, anxiety, stress, a lack of belief, tiredness, and so much more that makes me uncomfortable thinking about now. I never had a moment during that time when I didn't judge myself.

I wanted to feel significant as an athlete; I wanted to feel worthy of the uniforms I wore. My greatest fear has always been that I will remain a participant rather than a champion throughout life. I believed that failure and challenges would lead to a lack of recognition rather than championships, which caused me to sabotage many crucial moments throughout my life.

Today, I say, "I never played a down alone; I always had someone talking to me in my head."

I was my harshest critic. I was never good enough, and I always had to be the person I was expected to be. This mental mantra caused me to lose sixty pounds in one month after my college freshman football season in the worst way possible because I foolishly believed I wasn't the right body type for my position. I blacked out three times due to exhaustion and calorie deprivation from eating chicken and lettuce seven times a day while burning at least 6,000 calories in the same timeframe.

However, my need to do whatever it took to feel significant also led me to lift with the linemen, condition with the corners and safeties, and compete with the basketball team during the offseason. I even bench pressed 225 pounds twenty-six times, which was one of the highest rep amounts on the team, as a long snapper. I always saw one way to win and one way to lose, and the score was always dictated by powers outside of my control.

While some benefits came from this belief, so much more pain was caused by it. This toxic frame of mind was a slow death to my sports career; it caused me to underperform when it mattered most and led to me leaving the team after my junior year because I could no longer afford my living situation on student loans alone. I moved back home and began working to afford my education.

I expected to receive a scholarship after all the work I'd put in; I hoped the people who had told me I was going to be financially supported would keep their word. I expected everything and gave up all control in making it happen. When the entire coaching staff was let go, all the expectations I hung on to dissolved. I was broke—financially, physically, and mentally, wondering what would come next.

This shadow followed me into my life afterward, and I constantly found myself being the person who woke up tired, went to work, stared at the clock, and took every opportunity to bitch about everything to my loved ones, hoping that things would change. Things only got worse until I understood that I needed to manage the distractions within myself if I was ever to change the score in the games I was playing in life.

When I turned twenty-seven in September of 2019, I asked God to help me become the man I was meant to be so I could turn a corner in my life. I wasn't completely sure of who that was, but I knew for certain it wasn't who I had been. I promised myself that, when I graduated college, I would find my calling by helping others find success. I had never felt further from that promise and needed something to push me in the right direction.

The next day, the company I worked for let me know that the department was struggling, and they were consolidating teams. I was part of the group that would be let go immediately. At that time, my wife was five months pregnant. As a nanny who worked fifty or sixty-hour weeks, she made just enough to cover our mortgage and ramen. As you could imagine, I was at my lowest.

During that time, I was forced to sit with myself and face all the distractions that kept me company while fervently applying for work. What started as being pissed off changed to a feeling of detachment. I became numb to the frustration and anger. In this numbness, I began to rationalize why my life was the way it was, based on how I had made it that way, thanks to the book *Unf*ck Yourself* by Gary John Bishop. I then forgave myself, realizing that had I lost control in life, but I could get it back whenever I wanted to if it was important enough for me.

I began to see opportunities all around me, the biggest of which was that I deeply understood the athletic mindset. I knew the pitfalls that came with it through my own experiences, and I felt I could help others overcome or avoid those moments altogether. I was a young coach with a certification from the International Coaching Federation at the time and hadn't done much with it.

I knew that, if there was any time when I should put my learnings to the test, it was while I was struggling the most. If I was ever going to help others, I had to first transform myself into someone who knew how to consistently get the results I set out to achieve.

I decided to go all-in and work with an amazing coach I had connected with. I spent every last dollar I had, with the support of my wife, to work with them and commit to the process of becoming the champion I envisioned myself as.

Admittedly, I lied to the coach about how much money I had, saying I could pay their fee if it was broken down into payments. In reality, I could only afford the first payment. This is not an invitation for you to make the same risky financial gamble if it can be avoided. I made this choice with my wife because she knew I needed life to change like I needed air in my lungs; I knew I would succeed, and so did she. I just didn't understand how to make it happen and needed powerful guidance to realize my ambitions.

I had the drive, I had the willpower, and I had no other option but to take over the game. During the first month of my transformation,

I launched a podcast, networked with dozens of people, understood them deeply, and served them passionately. After five months of no work, no money, and almost 100 hours of interviewing for jobs and coaching opportunities, my son was born in January 2020.

At that time, I experienced the joy of completely surrendering to the moment. My wife and I had no money, no income, and no way to pay for the delivery of our incredible gift given to us. However, none of it mattered because I had put in the time and effort to take over the game. I knew the score would reflect the man I had become. Two days after his birth, I received calls and emails with job offers for more than twice as much as I had ever earned, and new clients accepted my proposals for far more than I had ever charged.

The first thing I did was thank God for removing the distractions from my life so that I could become the man I was meant to be. I thanked God for my wife's support and stability during a time of chaos in my life, for which I will be forever grateful. My mentor told me during that challenging time that my adventure would become an amazing story to tell and look back on once everything changed. Thanks, Mike; you were right.

In order to dictate the score in life, there are a few key areas you must be willing to explore. Each area stems from understanding that the results you want in life come from your ability to be the person who naturally achieves them. Why do we train, eat right, study our craft, shower, dress nice, and present ourselves with a confident persona as athletes?

The training, eating, and studying are there to maximize your potential for when you need to call on it. The other habits are there to minimize distractions, block out everything that doesn't serve you, and enforce the rule that only certain emotions and thoughts may join you during competition. This is all common practice with athletes in sports.

Why not take this same approach to all of life's performances? Well, we do in some ways. Showering, grooming, and dressing yourself are all hygienic routines designed to keep certain distractions out of your life while also helping you feel and look your best. However, there's a deeper mental aspect that all athletes can tap into when performing in any game of life.

I call the deeper level of this work "performance hygiene." The basis of this term is taking the concept that we grasp in sports and transitioning it to life afterward. It follows a simple three step process: get clean, get clear, get disciplined. These steps are the foundation of what I coach most people on, but they fit differently for every individual. Don't be afraid to adapt these steps and make them your own.

Getting clean is all about understanding why you're not where you want to be. It's about deeply embracing your distractions and the triggers that enable them.

Triggers are the events and situations that cause a conditioned response within us. The conditioned response is the distraction. For example, you mess up on a play, and your coach makes a critical comment about you needing to do better. Then, you start beating yourself up for your poor play, only to find yourself messing up even more. These cycles are what keep us from tapping into our full potential.

The trigger, in this case, is the coach criticizing you, while the distraction is your conditioned response to beat yourself up because of it. This pulls you away from being able to perform well. So, what can you do about this? First off, realize you're not the only one dealing with this challenge and stop beating yourself up about it. You must be objective to learn the trigger and response you currently have in order to decide on a new response that will serve you.

This process needs to be done in every area of your life. Think of it as a full spring cleaning of the mental hoarding you've been doing with conditioned responses that are detrimental to your success. If all you get from this chapter is the understanding that you must take time to look in the mirror, then I guarantee you'll be better off in life.

Getting clean is about being intentional when it comes to spending time with yourself so that you get more out of it. The cleaner you make yourself, the more potential you will naturally be able to tap into, and the easier it will be to hit your goals.

Now that you're clean, it's time to get clear. Without clear goals in your life, you have nothing to train for. As athletes, goals keep us motivated, aligned, and focused. In the absence of goals, we tend to do a ton of work and get nowhere. Clarity is about finding ways to direct your energy toward a single target. When you don't direct your energy, you're like a ten-watt lantern that projects light all around you in a short radius. This helps you for about two steps, but you aren't able to see very far ahead.

Focused energy toward a single target is like a ten-watt laser, which can melt steel over time. When you have clear focus and energy output, you'll melt barriers that stand in your way throughout life.

When you can set goals *and* be free from distractions, dreams become projects. To gain clarity, you have to know where you're currently at, which requires being honest and objective about your status in the present moment. Block out your subjective opinions and simply list the things in your life right now.

Aspects like your job title, salary, number of meaningful relationships, sense of fulfillment, and general health are the descriptors that will help you build a realistic view of where you currently are. If you have a moment, feel free to write those things down. When you have a clear picture of where you currently are, you can then build a view of where you want to be.

When you think about where you'd like to be, what kind of person would you describe yourself as? What are the values, habits, choices, and traits that make up your ideal self? Write those down if you haven't done so. What I want to point out here is that the different components of your life are all a reflection of the person you are.

If you are someone who lacks confidence right now, then your job, salary, and other things will reflect that. Your ideal self has a lifestyle that you can picture, which is just an external reflection of the internal traits you must embody for those things to naturally occur.

I promise you; your ideal self doesn't really want money; they want to become the person who provides massive value to others, and, therefore, people pay them for the value they provide. When you are clear about the person you need to be, you can then understand how to step into that clarity right now, which will start the countdown for when the lifestyle reflective of that person enters your life.

Don't feel overwhelmed if you see large gaps between where you are now and where you want to be. If you stand at the base of Mount Everest and stare at the top, you will probably think it's impossible to reach the summit. However, if you continuously look at the next step in front of you and know where those steps are taking you, you'll reach the top without realizing it.

Disciplines are the final step in the performance hygiene regimen. They are an athlete's superpower that gives you the endurance needed to continue dictating the score, game after game, throughout life. Every discipline is a practice associated with mastering yourself and mastering life. I say "practice" because they are daily habits you choose to implement in every scenario. The more you practice discipline in your life, the easier it becomes, and the more frequent your success will be.

Why do we love watching movies where the hero gets put into situations that seem overwhelmingly against them? It's because we know the character has disciplines deep down that will help them prevail against all odds and be unwavering in their pursuit of the results they desire. You can't help but root for someone who stands for something, and, therefore, will stand against other things.

Athletes naturally experience this in their training. If you want to win, you must be willing to stay the course. Deviating from the plan is not in the cards for you. One of the highest compliments an athlete can receive is praise for their discipline, as it is often given while the athlete is celebrating a win, a championship, or an unforgettable moment.

Disciplines that you can practice daily are self-awareness, conscious choice, acceptance, authenticity, and presence in the moment. Journey disciplines that you practice over longer periods of time are trusting the process, 100 percent energetic engagement, fearlessness, and confidence. Finally, the discipline you practice and give to others is your connection to yourself and to others.

These disciplines are powerful and require dedication to stick to. However, they are the vehicle you will use to consistently drive toward peak performance and a legacy you can be proud of that will inspire others long after your time is up. No one will ever be upset with you for being a driven individual when your goals and disciplines are clear. If they are, it's because they are upset with themselves for not doing the same.

You have more power than you realize. You're closer to making your dreams a reality than you are to having them turn to dust. You have the unique ability to change the world in a way only you are capable of. Sometimes, it's easy to see the impact we can have on the world, and other times it can seem blurry. If you feel like things are more difficult than they should be, know that it is okay to ask for help.

You've spent your whole life working with coaches, specialists, and teammates. This habit does not have to stop when your athletic career ends. If anything, the habit should be taken up a notch. By asking for help when you need it, you can ensure your path to success by working with people who help you consistently tap into your inner champion.

I believe that we can all take over the game we are playing, at any time, through an unexplainable force within us. Or, we can choose to be buried beneath a sea of distractions. I believe that you can control what creates your world—your mindset. I believe that you can be unstoppable.

ABOUT KEEGAN

Keegan LaMar is a husband, father, coach, and former D1 collegiate football player. After working in the business world, he decided to shift his focus from building company brands and stories to helping individuals write theirs. His passion for coaching comes from a lifetime of incredible relationships and experiences with people. Keegan started his coaching company, LaMar Coaching LLC., in 2018, but would say that he has been doing this his entire life.

As a writer, podcast host, and coach, Keegan believes that people can control their world when they master their mindset. He lives by a simple formula: Performance = Potential − Distractions. He uses this formula to transform his clients' lives from constantly searching for a win in their life, to success being a natural occurrence.

Keegan works with performance-minded individuals to help them create impact in their own lives and the lives of others through mastering their unique approach to performance. He is a certified professional coach through the International Coaching Federation and has a certification in Core Energy Performance Dynamics as well. Keegan is also the host of the *Unstoppable Mindset* podcast, a show dedicated to understanding how high-performing mindsets work through both challenging and prosperous times so people can learn how to uncover their own unique approach to peak performance in sports, business, and life.

As Keegan looks ahead, he aims to arm the next generation of leaders with the foundational mental performance information he did not have access to until later in life, so they can unlock an unstoppable mindset earlier than most people ever do.

Connect with Keegan:
Website: www.lamarcoaching.com
Email:keegan@lamarcoaching.com
Instagram: @lamarcoaching

CONCLUSION
BY CORY CAMP

Who we are can't simply be defined by what we do. By doing so, we shortchange ourselves and our true potential. As you've seen throughout each of the stories in this book, peak performance is ultimately a simple concept, but it is not easy in practice. It begins with being yourself.

Who we truly are is our strongest superpower, and only we are the best at being ourselves. The more we lean into that strength, the more we can grow and evolve as people.

Despite what people might tell you, there is no one way to be yourself or find your true identity. You saw that throughout the pages of this book. The beauty is that you have an opportunity to create your own lane. You're at your best when you're playing your game, not someone else's. That means from here on out, you have an opportunity to wake up each day and choose how you're going to play.

"
Who we truly are is our strongest superpower
"

Will it be on your terms? Or the terms of those around you? As a Forever Athlete, you know what choice you get to make each day. While that choice might not be common among most people, you've gotten here because you're not like most people.

We encourage you to keep making the simple choice of being you in every situation you find yourself in. We're here for you each step of the way.

We invite you to connect with the other Forever Athletes of the world at www.foreverathletela.com and enjoy two months of our Varsity membership with code "FAR Book" at checkout.

Together we go FAR.

Yours in growth,
Cory & The Forever Athlete Team

Made in the USA
Middletown, DE
24 March 2022

63120127R00146